Teach Yourself®

Get Started with Origami

Robert Harbin

For UK order enquiries: please contact Bookpoint Ltd, 130 Milton
Park, Abingdon, Oxon OX14 4SB. Telephone: +44 (0) 1235 827720.
Fax: +44 (0) 1235 400454. Lines are open 09.00–17.00, Monday to
Saturday, with a 24-hour message answering service. Details about
our titles and how to order are available at www.teachyourself.com

For USA order enquiries: please contact McGraw-Hill Customer
Services, PO Box 545, Blacklick, OH 43004-0545, USA.
Telephone: 1-800-722-4726. Fax: 1-614-755-5645.

For Canada order enquiries: please contact McGraw-Hill
Ryerson Ltd, 300 Water St, Whitby, Ontario L1N 9B6, Canada.
Telephone: 905 430 5000. Fax: 905 430 5020.

Long renowned as the authoritative source for self-guided
learning – with more than 50 million copies sold worldwide –
the *Teach Yourself* series includes over 500 titles in the fields of
languages, crafts, hobbies, business, computing and education.

British Library Cataloguing in Publication Data: a catalogue record
for this title is available from the British Library.

Library of Congress Catalog Card Number: on file.

First published in UK 1992 by Hodder Education, part of
Hachette UK, 338 Euston Road, London NW1 3BH.

First published in US 1992 by The McGraw-Hill Companies, Inc.

This edition published 2010.

Previously published as *Teach Yourself Origami*.

The *Teach Yourself* name is a registered trade mark of
Hodder Headline.

Typeset by MPS Limited, A Macmillan Company.

Printed in Great Britain for Hodder Education, an Hachette UK
Company, 338 Euston Road, London NW1 3BH, by CPI Cox &
Wyman, Reading, Berkshire RG1 8EX.

The publisher has used its best endeavours to ensure that the URLs
for external websites referred to in this book are correct and active
at the time of going to press. However, the publisher and the
author have no responsibility for the websites and can make no
guarantee that a site will remain live or that the content will remain
relevant, decent or appropriate.

Hachette UK's policy is to use papers that are natural, renewable
and recyclable products and made from wood grown in sustainable
forests. The logging and manufacturing processes are expected to
conform to the environmental regulations of the country of origin.

Impression number   10 9 8 7 6 5 4 3 2 1
Year   2014 2013 2012 2011 2010

To Neal Elias and Fred Rohm

Contents

Foreword to the new edition

The Teach Yourself title *Get Started with Origami* was first published in a hard-backed edition in 1968 and was an instant success. The following year it was published in a paperback edition. During the next few years it was joined by three more volumes in the series and became generally known as 'Origami 1'. It was translated into several languages including French, German, Italian and Hebrew.

In 1980 'Origami 1' was revised and reissued. A new historical introduction and an updated bibliography were added and the name *Teach Yourself Origami* was reintroduced. It was revised again in 1992 and provided with a new bibliography and redrawn, clearer diagrams.

Robert Harbin died on 12 July 1978 and he bequeathed his copyrights to the British Origami Society, of which he had been made the President when the Society was founded in 1967. Since his death his book has remained popular and is still looked on with affection as one of the best introductions to the art of paperfolding, including as it does, an interesting diversity of models ranging from the simple and traditional to the more unusual and complex.

Now, *Get Started with Origami* has been updated once more. Several new models have been chosen by David Brill, the Chairman of the British Origami Society. A postscript has been added to the historical introduction and David Brill has compiled a new bibliography, which points readers towards the best modern writers of origami books.

I hope that for many years to come Robert Harbin's classic book of origami in this new edition will continue to instruct and fascinate folders, experienced and newcomers alike.

David Lister
President of the British Origami Society

Meet the author

Writing a book, whatever the subject, is always a laborious task for me. But writing this addition to the *Teach Yourself* series has been a real pleasure, because I am anxious to introduce as many as possible to the world of origami, which has given me so much enjoyment.

The main task has been to design the illustrations, because without them there could not be a book. Diagrams take a long time to prepare because, fold by fold, the three-dimensional paper model must be reduced to a two-dimensional drawing on a flat sheet of paper. And the drawing must be clear and accurate if the student is to understand how to produce the finished model from it.

It could be argued, I suppose, that origami has an end product that is not worth keeping. Nothing could be further from the truth. At the time of writing, I have a delightful collection of the world's best paper folds, carefully stored in transparent envelopes, which are in turn mounted on a sheet of black board. This way, they are ready to be produced and shown quickly – and they *are* produced and shown, at the slightest provocation!

If this art form captures you, as it has certainly captured me and many others, you will discover that it brings with it a new dimension in enjoyment, which is infinite in its variety and unrivalled in its capacity to make you relax and forget everything else.

Robert Harbin

A short history of origami

'Origami' is a Japanese word which simply means 'paper-folding'. It was adopted first in English and then in other languages in recognition of the long tradition of the Japanese people for folding paper.

The Chinese invented paper, probably before the birth of Christ, and we can only guess that they were the first to fold paper. But we do know that by the twelfth century AD paper was used in Japan for folding ceremonial wrappers ('tsutsumu') for storage of household goods, such as herbs, and for gifts, especially gifts of flowers, where each kind of flower had its special wrapper. The present-day Japanese custom of attaching to gifts small tokens of folded paper called 'noshi' is a relic of this ceremonial paper-folding; some other paper-folding customs have also survived.

Apart from occasional far-from-clear references to paper animals, birds and flowers, the earliest informative records we have of recreational, as opposed to ceremonial, paper-folding are two Japanese books, the *Senbazuru Orikata* and the *Chushingura Orikata*, both dating from 1797. The first describes how to fold connected groups and chains of paper cranes (very similar to the classic flapping bird on page 98) and the second shows how to fold a series of characters from a popular play. These paper dolls resemble somewhat Robert Harbin's Japanese Lady and Gentleman on pages 168 to 172. The folding in these two books is much more advanced than the simple folds familiar to children round the world and its presupposes a long tradition of paper-folding in Japan before 1800.

The little paper dolls appear again in the *Kan no mado*, a manuscript encyclopedia believed to date from the middle of the nineteenth century. This contains several ceremonial folds and also some elaborately folded animals and insects which use extensive cutting: something which would not be acceptable today.

As modern creative origami avoids cutting it does not derive directly from the tradition of the *Kan no mado* and it is the flapping bird itself which lies at the heart of the modern development of the art. This remarkable folded toy was brought to Europe from Japan about 1880. Japanese stage magicians and also educationalists are believed to have been involved. The flapping bird was quickly absorbed into the small European repertoire of children's folds, which already had a long tradition. European folds were, however, for the most part, restricted to a few simple hats, boxes and boats, together with the salt cellar (page 29) and what Robert Harbin called the 'multiform' series of folds (pages 81–91). Another multiform figure not included in this book is the curious 'hobby horse', which is known in Spain as the *pajarita*, meaning 'little bird'. The Spanish philosopher Miguel de Unanumo (1864–1936) took a delight in childish things, including paper-folding, and was fascinated by the *pajarita*. Later, by manipulating the bird base (pages 91–7), which was the foundation for the flapping bird, he created a series of somewhat angular birds and animals, which nevertheless greatly extended the possibilities of paper-folding. His most significant discovery was the sideways twist of the flaps of the bird base, which is also used in Yoshizawa's pigeon (page 101). A small group of followers of Unanumo came into being and the praying moor (page 107) is an example of their work. The Spanish tradition spread to South America and culminated in the vast analytical work of Dr. Solorzano Sagredo and the delicately creative work of his pupil, the late Ligia Montoya of Argentina, two of whose simple models are the tropical birds on pages 137–41.

In Japan, Isao Honda made collections of traditional and modern origami and new books began to appear, notably those by Michio Uchiyama and his son Kosho Uchiyama. Then, quite independently of Unanumo, Akira Yoshizawa made similar discoveries about the possibilities of the bird base. Some of his work was published by Isao Honda in 1944. After the Second World War, Yoshizawa began to publish his own books and articles and Japanese paper-folding entered a new period of creativity. Akira Yoshizawa's ingenuity is matched by his incomparable skill in bringing his models to life and he continues to dominate the art in Japan.

Before the war, paper-folding in English-speaking countries had been limited to the traditional children's folds, but in the 1950s it began to develop through the efforts of three people: Gershon Legman and Lillian Oppenheimer of the United States and Robert Harbin of Britain. Curiously none of them claimed to be a creative folder. Gershon Legman compiled a bibliography and also established contacts with both Akira Yoshizawa and Ligia Montoya. Lillian Oppenheimer publicized origami and founded the Origami Center of America in New York. She puts folders in touch with one another and made many books available, including some in Spanish and Japanese. Robert Harbin demonstrated paper-folding on television for the first time in 1955, and in 1956 he published his excellent book *Paper Magic*, which summarized the art and for a time became the standard manual in English.

The work of these three people brought together for the first time many people who had been folding paper for their own amusement in isolation and the newly available books inspired a generation of creative folders, especially in America where Fred Rohm, Neal Elias, Robert Neale, George Rhoads and Jack Skillman devised new techniques and basic folds which opened up possibilities for paper-folding undreamed of even in Japan. For a time the bird base and its related folds, the fish base and frog base, remained the foundations for folding but they were soon joined by more complex versions including multiple and 'blinz' bird and frog bases. Before long entirely new ideas emerged including the 'box-folding' of Dr Emanual Mooser of Switzerland and 'box-pleating' developed especially by Neal Elias.

Despite the influence of Robert Harbin, paper-folding in Britain lagged behind until the British Origami Society was formed in 1967 from a group of folders whom Lillian Oppenheimer had put in touch with each other. The Society developed slowly but its membership grew significantly following the original publication of *Teach Yourself Origami* in 1968. Since then the Society's magazine *British Origami* has become one of the world's leading journals on the subject.

In the 1970s, just when some began to think that the limits of folding had been reached, members of the British Origami Society broke new ground and produced a large number of greatly varied models of remarkable ingenuity, widely differing in style, sometimes mechanical, sometimes artistic. The classic bird and frog bases were now abandoned by creative folders and new, specialized bases were developed that were uniquely appropriate for the model to be folded.

The new Western techniques were taken back to Japan, where a younger generation of Japanese have combined the mechanical virtuosity of the West with the delicate artistry of the East. Dokuohtei Nakano and Yoshihide Momotani were two of the best-known among many new Japanese folders. Another Japanese, Shuzo Fujimoto, made new discoveries about the geometrical possibilities of folding, which he developed with great ingenuity. Many of his ideas await exploration by other folders.

In the 1980s complex bases were further developed in the United States by John Montroll, Robert Lang, Stephen Weiss and Peter Engel and in Japan by Jun Maekawa. While their style was too technical for some people's tastes, their folding of anatomically correct insects and sea creatures, complete with all their legs and other appendages, finally proved that the possibilities of an uncut square of paper were limitless.

Contrasted with the 'technical school', the British Paul Jackson's minimalist style uses creases to tension the paper and create a kind of uncut paper-sculpture. Another Briton, John S. Smith, devised 'pure-land' folding, which used only simple mountain and valley folds. It began as an attempt to find simple folds for children and handicapped people and ended as an intellectual exercise. Folding does not have to be complex to retain its beauty and fascination.

The 1980s showed the continuing vitality of paper-folding in other ways. 'Modular origami' (the linking of many identical folded units to form composite models) became popular and was exemplified by the immaculate work of Miss Tomoko Fuse of Japan. The First International Meeting of Origami Science and Technology was held at Ferrera in Italy in 1989; at the meeting a distinguished gathering of scientists and mathematicians explored the awesome depths of origami geometry. There has also been a revived awareness of the value of paper-folding as a therapy for the disabled and handicapped and in child education, where it is employed not only as a manual exercise and for stimulation of geometrical awareness in the tradition of Friedrich Fröebel (1782–1852), the originator of the kindergarten, but also in less obvious fields such as the development of language ability and as an aid to conceptualization.

The happiest thing about paper-folding is that it has grown as a truly international movement and folders in North and South America, Britain, France, Italy, Germany and many other countries are in regular contact and frequently travel long distances to visit the conventions of each other's societies. New discoveries are shared and exhibitions are held to which contributions are sent from all over the world. Groups have now been formed in eastern Europe and paper-folders from Russia have already visited England.

When we practise origami we pay tribute to the memory of Robert Harbin, the master stage-magician, who became so enthralled by the world contained in a mere square of paper that he decided to tell everyone about his discovery. He freely admitted that conjuring tricks depended on deception, but said that paper-folding really was magic. He would surely have been happy to watch the continuing growth of his 'paper-magic' and its spread to the far corners of the Earth. It was Robert Harbin's heartfelt wish that his beloved origami should ever continue to bring peace and friendship to all people and by sharing in that hope, paper-folders will honour his memory in the way that he himself would have cherished.

Postscript

Since this introduction was last revised, origami has continued to
flourish and to grow both in richness and in its geographical extent.
Today it reaches all the corners of the earth. In eastern Europe
there is now a lively interest in origami, especially in Hungary and
in Russia where there are not only active groups in Moscow and
St. Petersburg, but even in remote Siberia. Paperfolding has also
grown rapidly in many parts of South America – in Venezuela,
Colombia, Peru and Brazil – all of them far from the early South
American development of paper-folding in Argentina.

The art of paper-folding itself continues to develop in ways that
Robert Harbin could not possibly have foreseen back in 1968.
Both the Japanese and the Americans have taken complex origami
to new heights, so that there is now scarcely anything that cannot
be folded from an uncut sheet of paper. Computer programs have
been devised to help the process. Modular folding has continued
to be popular, as new techniques have been discovered. There has
been a flurry of books about folding paper money, especially in
the United States, where the unusual 3×7 proportions of the
dollar bill have been a particular challenge to folders.

A remarkable development has been the creative work of sculptors
who have used paperfolding as their medium. This trend has
been particularly strong in France with the textured work of
Jean-Claude Correia; the imaginative creations of Vincent Floderer,
whose forms are inspired by mushrooms, trees and coral; and
the magnificent sculptured heads of Eric Joisel, whose techniques
nevertheless remain firmly based in simple techniques of origami.
Paul Jackson, too, has used the technique of 'cross-pleating' to
create exquisite sculptural bowls.

The scope of origami has widened in other ways. Two more
international meetings of scientific origami were held in Otsu,
Japan, in 1994 and in California in 2001, and were attended
by scientists, mathematicians and paperfolders from all over

the world. At these meetings science, mathematics and art were uniquely united. We are learning much more about the complex mathematics of origami and about its application to scientific research. Some of the topics studied, such as the folding of proteins, seem exotic indeed!

There has also been an increase in the application of Origami as a therapy for both psychological and physical purposes. Paper-folding used with proper understanding is a great healer. The educational paper-folding of Friedrich Fröebel suffered an eclipse during the first half of the twentieth century because it was considered to be uncreative. But now origami is again being accepted as a valuable educational medium demonstrating its effectiveness, not only in co-ordinating hand and eye, but also in contributing to the formation of the deeper processes of the mind and psyche. International conferences on origami in Education and Therapy were held in Birmingham, England, in 1991 and in New York in 1995.

The years since the first publication of *Teach Yourself Origami* have seen a revolution in world communication. As in every other field, television, air travel and more recently the Internet have made the world a much smaller place for origami and have greatly increased communication between paper-folders as they have crossed national boundaries and oceans to attend the conventions that are held in many countries every year. But the greatest change has been the influence of the Internet.

Paper-folders have a natural affinity with computers and have not been slow to exploit them. The Origami Internet List ('Origami-L') is a busy international group, bringing together folders from all countries. Other Internet lists serve other languages and special interests. The number of websites devoted to origami multiplies daily and every aspect of folding, paper or otherwise, can be found somewhere on the World Wide Web, ranging from the hidden obscurities of Japanese traditional folding to the theoretical folding of paper in multiple mathematical dimensions.

During all of these changes, the simpler, familiar kind of paper-folding has continued to fascinate the great majority of paper-folders. Robert Harbin's *Get Started with Origami* remains stimulating and yet its standard is attainable by the average folder. His models range from age-old traditional favourites, to models that take their style from more recently-discovered techniques. *Get Started with Origami* remains a valuable introduction for every paper-folder. Robert Harbin's reputation lives on and there is a constant demand for his books to be reprinted 25 years after his death. He would have been surprised and delighted to find that he still continues to play such a substantial part in introducing his beloved origami to new generations who could never have met him. He would know his ambition to bring origami to the world had been fulfilled.

David Lister
26 July 2002

The essentials of origami

Most beginners are not able to follow diagrams and instructions easily and successfully, however carefully they may have been planned. As a rule, origami illustrators try to cram into each page as much information as possible. This practice is welcomed by the enthusiast and the expert, because it means that the book will be able to explain a large number of models. Unfortunately, though, a page filled with diagrams completely bewilders most beginners.

I have borne this in mind while preparing this book, and you will see that the earlier pages have been designed with no more than two or three diagrams on each page. All the diagrams are clearly drawn, and contain instructions and symbols to give you all possible help, and to explain the mainly standard models which bring you in touch with most of the basic folds.

A basic fold is a fold from which many models can be made. There are many basic folds, both ancient and modern, but this book will introduce you to just enough to give you a good groundwork with which to begin.

Look at the first fold illustrated in the book, and notice how instructions are placed on the parts to be folded: FOLD THIS SIDE DOWN, and then TO HERE, and so on. The instructions are made to work for you. Later in the book, the instructions are placed next to the diagrams, and not on them, because it is assumed that by then you will have become familiar with the different processes.

Always fold carefully, accurately and neatly. If you fold carelessly, the result will be disastrous.

Study each diagram showing the complete folded model first, and only then, place your origami paper in front of you and make your first fold.

When you make a fold, always crease the paper firmly with the back of your thumbnail. Good creases make folding easy, and are an invaluable guide later in the model, when you are making a series of folds.

Pre-creasing is an important feature. Consider, for example, the Japanese lady (page 171). This model was sent to Samuel Randlett, who immediately used the idea to produce his fine fish (page 173). Notice how he pre-creases the paper he uses so that everything folds into place at the right moment.

Before you make a reverse fold, pre-crease the paper by folding the whole thickness before opening the paper and making the fold (see Reverse folds).

Notice how paper coloured on one side is used to get the maximum effect for each model. The subject of paper is an important one. Origami paper should be strong, thin and suitable coloured. But if you cannot find special origami paper, almost any paper may be used.

If you are instructed to use a square of paper, make sure that it really is square, and that a rectangle is a true rectangle. Most of the models in this book are based on squares of paper, but there is no regular rule about this, as all shapes of paper can be used, according to the model's needs. See, for example, the Ornithonimus (page 177) and Aladdin's lamp (page 180).

Origami is not a simple art. To the expert, it is a challenge to the eye, the brain and the fingers – a wonderful mental and physical therapy.

When you fold one of the decorations explained in this book, you will find that by altering this or that fold you can invent endless shapes. In fact, you can improvize for hours.

When you have mastered the basic folds, you will then be equipped to produce figures and shapes of your own inventions. Have something in mind, and then consider the best base from which to start. You will notice that there are three different ways in which to make a penguin. The penguin seems to be a favourite subject, and almost every folder has a go at it.

Watch out for terms like squash fold. It is so named because you do just that – squash the part indicated so that the sides bulge and it flattens, in most cases symmetrically.

Study the petal folds, the rabbit's ears and the various bases, and try to remember what they are. If you get stuck, have a look at the Contents and refer to the pages concerned.

You will notice that certain procedures are used over and over again. You will soon get used to these and be able to carry them out automatically.

When you have folded everything in the first half of the book, you will find that more and more diagrams begin to appear on each page, and that the symbols begin to play a bigger part than the instructions. Decoration 2 (page 161) has been included as an exercise so try to make this up using the symbols only.

Finally – take it slowly; fold carefully, neatly and accurately. And START AT THE BEGINNING!

A note on symbols

The symbols used in this book are based on Akira Yoshizawa's code of lines and arrows. Symbols will become second nature to you when folding as they are easy to acquire.

The moment you see a line of dashes, you know that the paper must be valley folded along that line. When you see a line of dashes and dots, you recognize the sign for a mountain fold. To make a mountain fold, you naturally turn the paper upside down and make a valley fold.

Arrows show the directions in which you must fold: left, right, up, down, in front, behind and into.

You will notice one arrow which shows that a drawing has been enlarged for clarity. Another arrow indicates that a model must be opened out (see Samuel Randlett's fish, page 173). My own little black arrow indicates that you must sink, press, squeeze or push in at certain points.

The symbols are in fact self-explanatory. They are simple common sense, and can be learnt in about ten minutes.

Try to use the symbols only and ignore explanations. This will help you when you come to read Japanese origami books.

International origami symbols

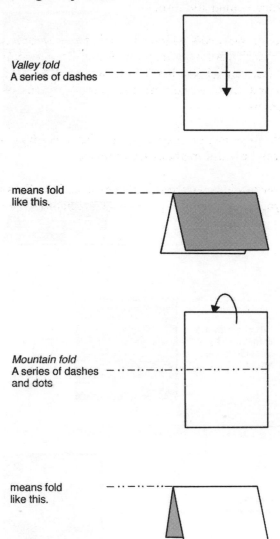

Valley fold
A series of dashes

means fold
like this.

Mountain fold
A series of dashes
and dots

means fold
like this.

Study the symbols carefully

If a drawing
was marked
with these symbols

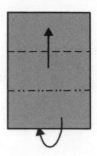

the result
should be
this.

When a drawing
is followed by
this little looped
arrow

turn the
model over.

Symbols take the place of instructions

This black arrow

means push in.

Thin lines mean creases.

This symbol

means

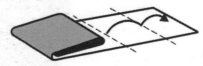

fold over and over.

Make this water bomb base and preliminary fold

If a drawing is
marked like this

you make this
water bomb base.

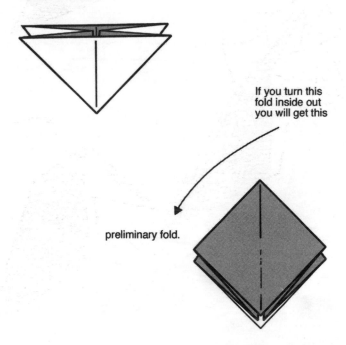

If you turn this
fold inside out
you will get this

preliminary fold.

How to make a reverse fold

Reverse fold 1

Note how paper is
marked. Crease
along the mark.
Now reverse fold
as shown

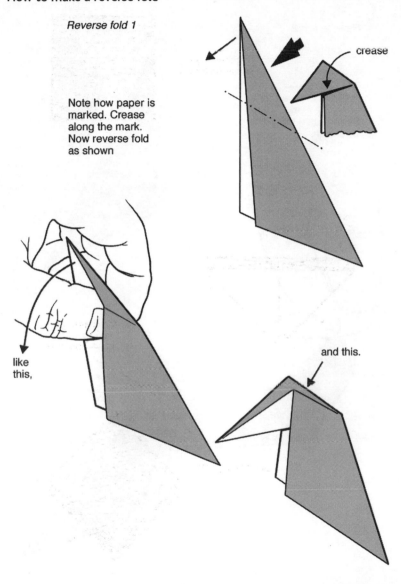

crease

like
this,

and this.

An 'outside' reverse fold

Reverse fold 2

Note how paper is
marked. Crease
along the mark.
Now reverse fold
as shown.

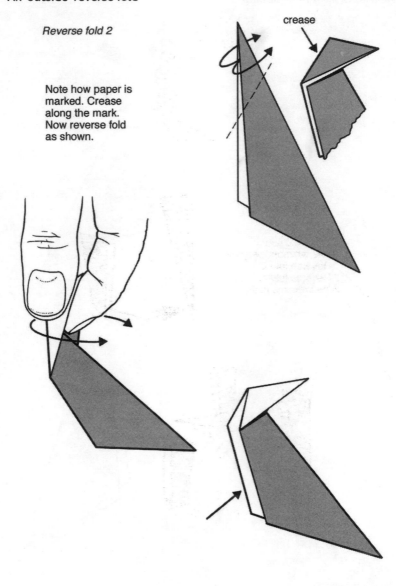

crease

How to make a foot

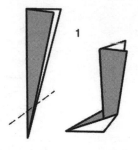

How to fold feet
(birds, animals, people).
1 Reverse fold 2.
2 Reverse fold 1.
3 Two reverse folds.

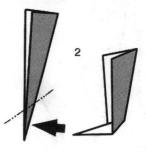

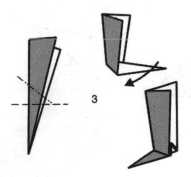

How to make a bird's head

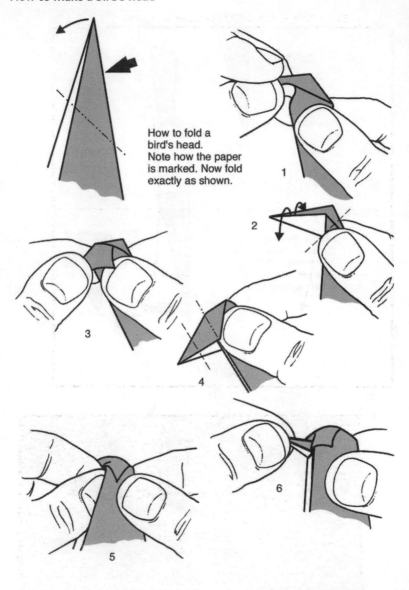

How to fold a bird's head. Note how the paper is marked. Now fold exactly as shown.

1

2

3

4

5

6

House: a simple Japanese fold

Start with the white side of the paper facing you.

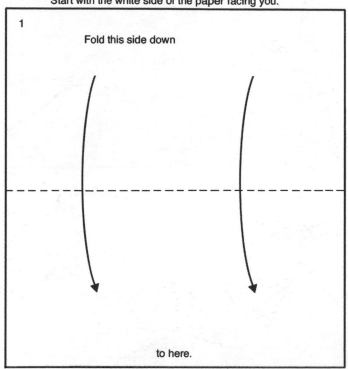

1

Fold this side down

to here.

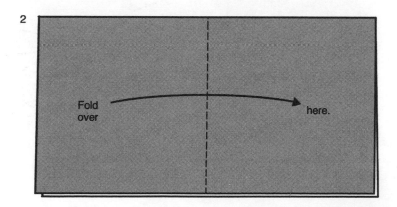

2

Fold over

here.

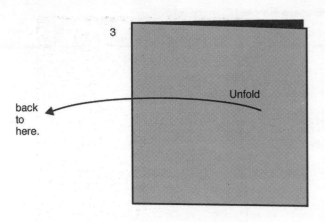

3

Unfold

back
to
here.

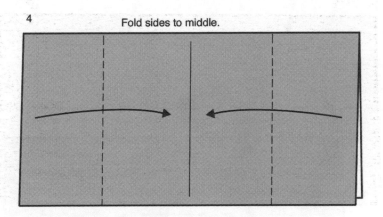

4   Fold sides to middle.

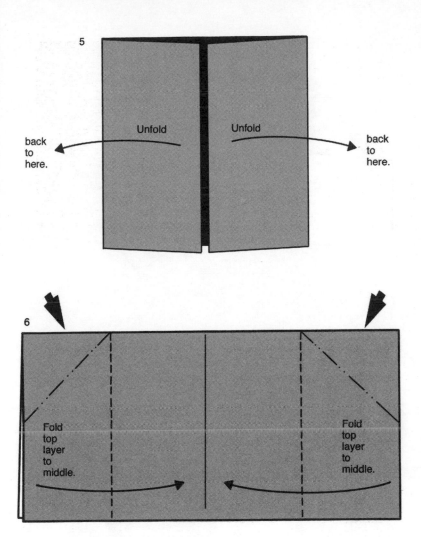

5

back
to
here.

Unfold

Unfold

back
to
here.

6

Fold
top
layer
to
middle.

Fold
top
layer
to
middle.

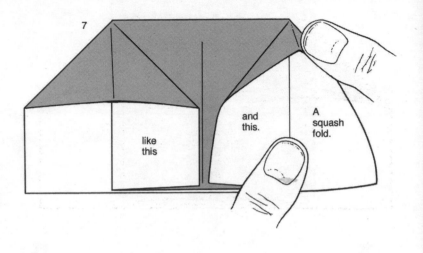

7

like
this

and
this.

A
squash
fold.

Now draw doors and windows.

8

G.I. cap
Start with house fold.

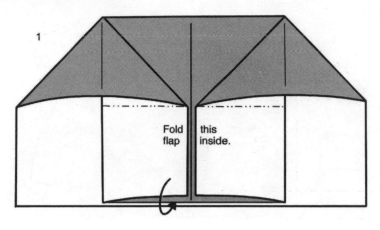

1

Fold this
flap inside.

Now –
turn the
model over

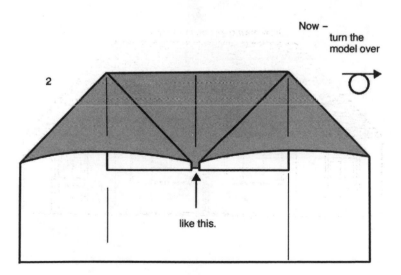

2

like this.

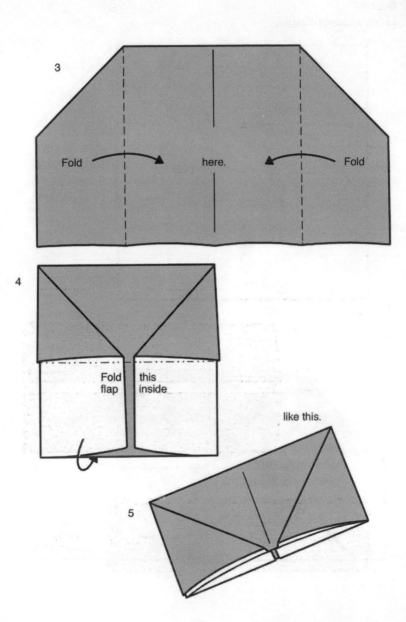

3

Fold → here. ← Fold

4

Fold flap | this inside

like this.

5

26

Boat

Use a square of paper.

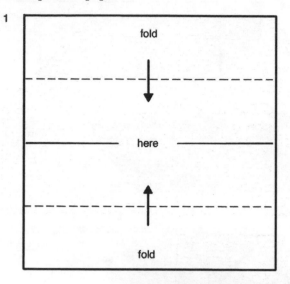

1

fold

here ————

fold

First crease along the middle.

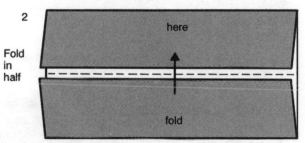

2

Fold in half

here

fold

like this.

3

Now fold the two corners up

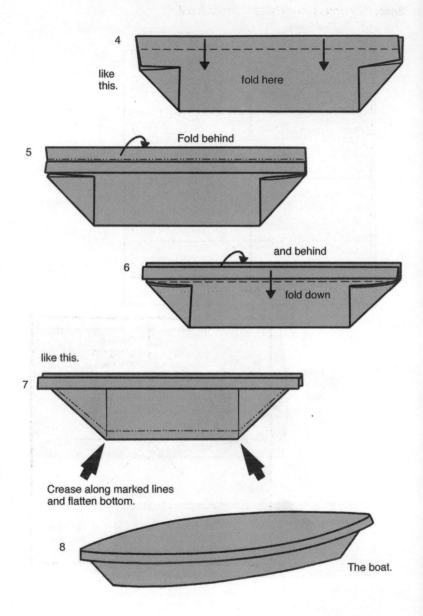

4

like
this.

fold here

5

Fold behind

6

and behind

fold down

like this.

7

Crease along marked lines
and flatten bottom.

8

The boat.

Salt cellar and colour changer: traditional

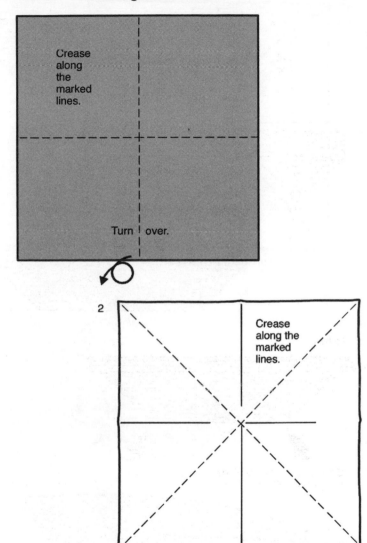

1. Crease along the marked lines.

   Turn over.

2. Crease along the marked lines.

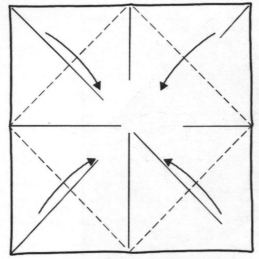

Now fold the corners in

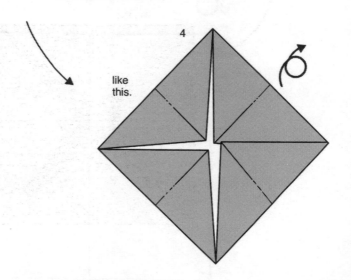

like
this.

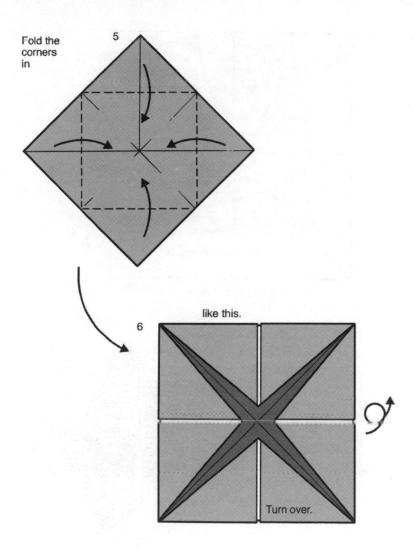

Fold the corners in

5

like this.

6

Turn over.

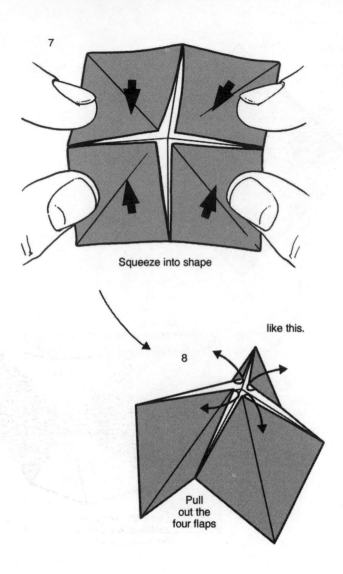

7

Squeeze into shape

like this.

8

Pull
out the
four flaps

9   like this.

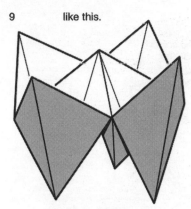

The salt cellar.

10

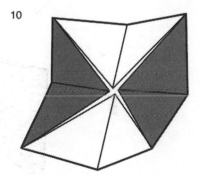

This is the salt cellar
upside down. Colour
the areas shown

Colour changer

11   to make
the colour
changer.

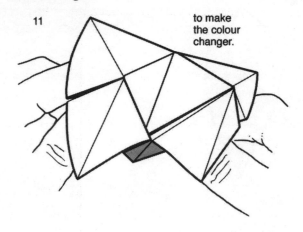

And this
shows how you
make it work.

12

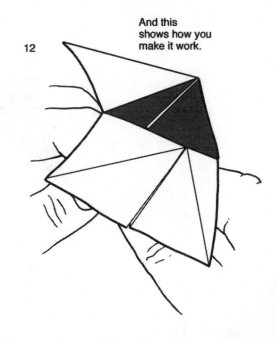

34

Spanish box: Spanish, originally Japanese

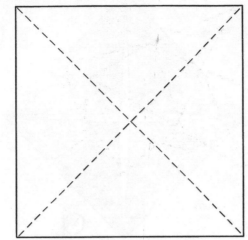

Crease along the marked lines.

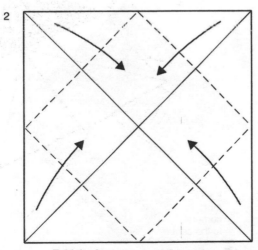

Fold the four corners to the centre.

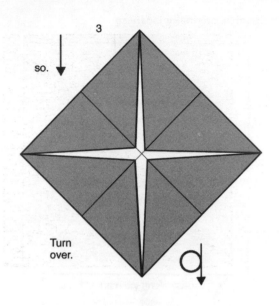

3

so.

Turn
over.

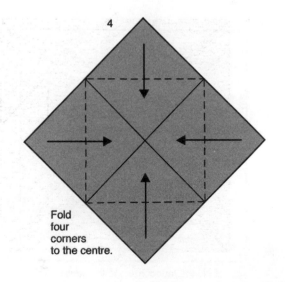

4

Fold
four
corners
to the centre.

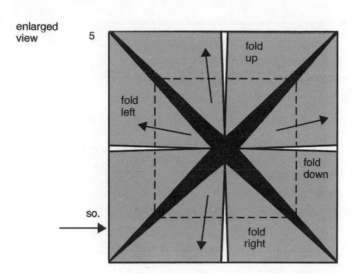

enlarged view

5

fold up

fold left

fold down

so.

fold right

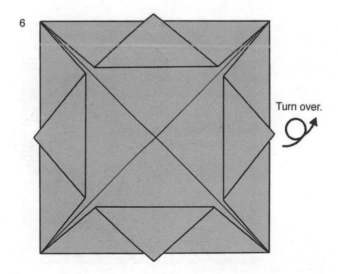

6

Turn over.

7

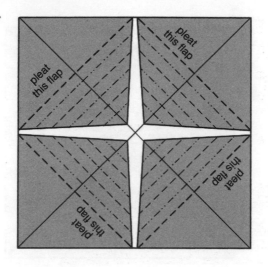

pleat this flap

pleat this flap

pleat this flap

pleat this flap

8

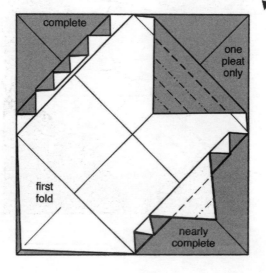

complete

one pleat only

first fold

nearly complete

9

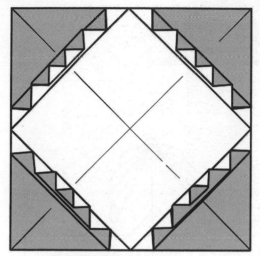

Completed pleats.

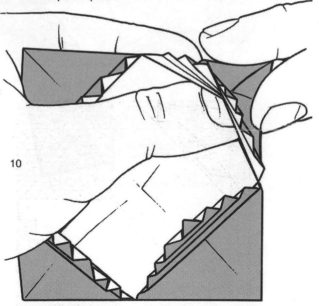

10

A ketchup bottle should fit this.

Push left thumb into each
corner and press together
on the outside until the
fancy box is completed

so.

11

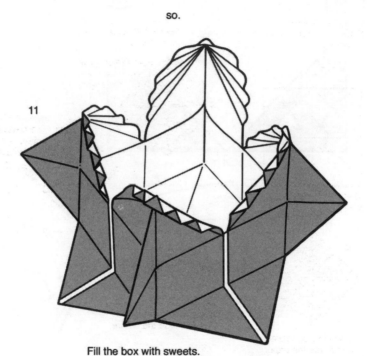

Fill the box with sweets.

Traditional Japanese box and lid

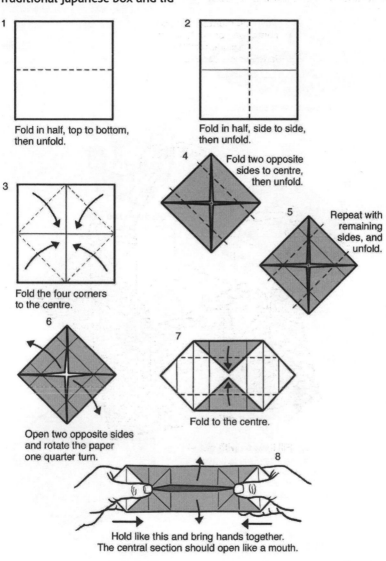

1 Fold in half, top to bottom, then unfold.

2 Fold in half, side to side, then unfold.

3 Fold the four corners to the centre.

4 Fold two opposite sides to centre, then unfold.

5 Repeat with remaining sides, and unfold.

6 Open two opposite sides and rotate the paper one quarter turn.

7 Fold to the centre.

8 Hold like this and bring hands together. The central section should open like a mouth.

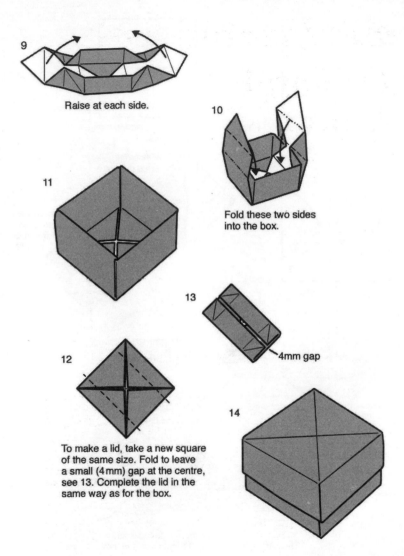

9

Raise at each side.

10

Fold these two sides
into the box.

11

13

4mm gap

12

14

To make a lid, take a new square
of the same size. Fold to leave
a small (4mm) gap at the centre,
see 13. Complete the lid in the
same way as for the box.

Turban, or Japanese purse
Use a rectangular piece of paper.

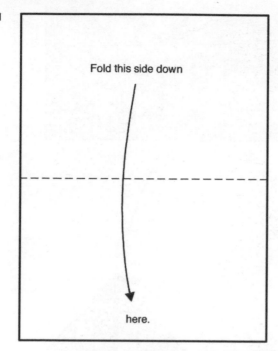

Fold this side down

here.

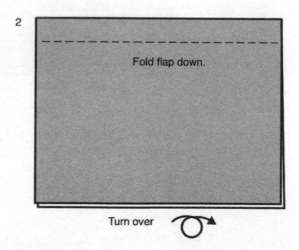

Fold flap down.

Turn over

3

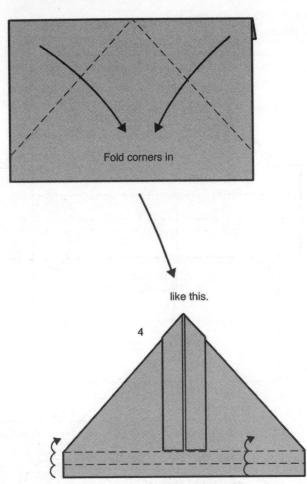

Fold corners in

like this.

4

Fold this flap over
twice.

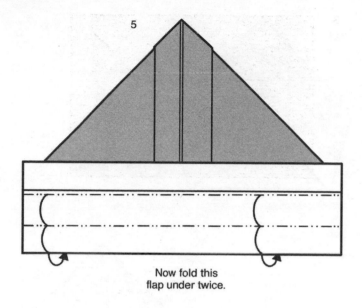

5

Now fold this
flap under twice.

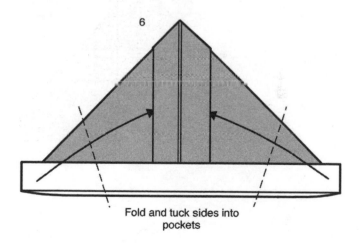

6

Fold and tuck sides into
pockets

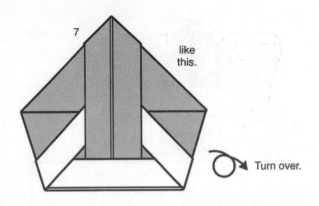

7

like
this.

Turn over.

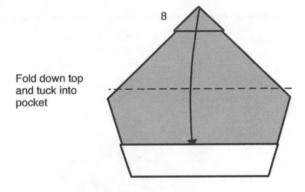

8

Fold down top
and tuck into
pocket

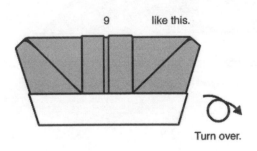

9   like this.

Turn over.

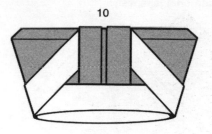

The turban complete.

Try this with
a sheet of
newspaper.

Samurai hat: traditional Japanese

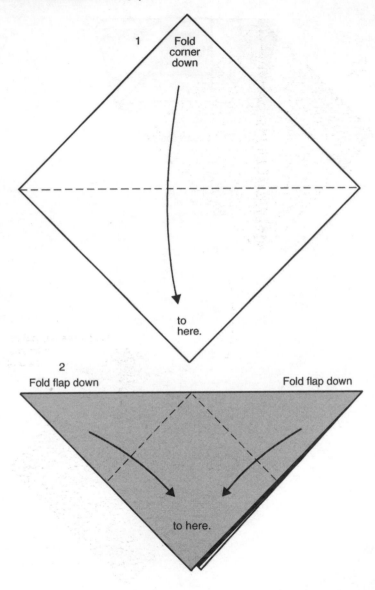

1
Fold
corner
down

to
here.

2
Fold flap down

Fold flap down

to here.

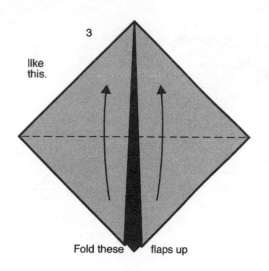

3

like this.

Fold these flaps up

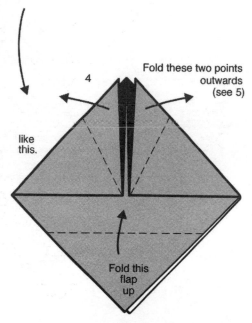

4

like this.

Fold these two points outwards (see 5)

Fold this flap up

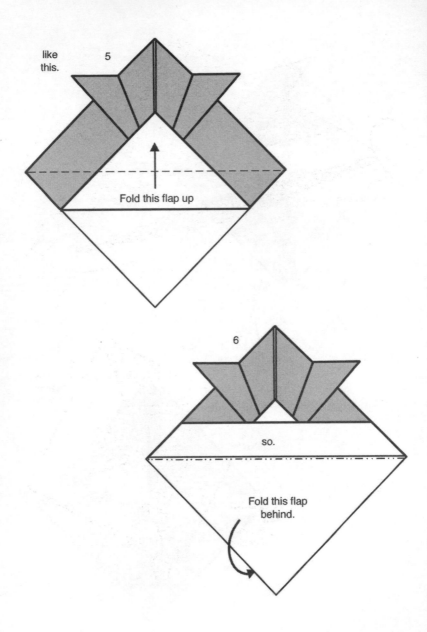

like this.

5

Fold this flap up

6

so.

Fold this flap
behind.

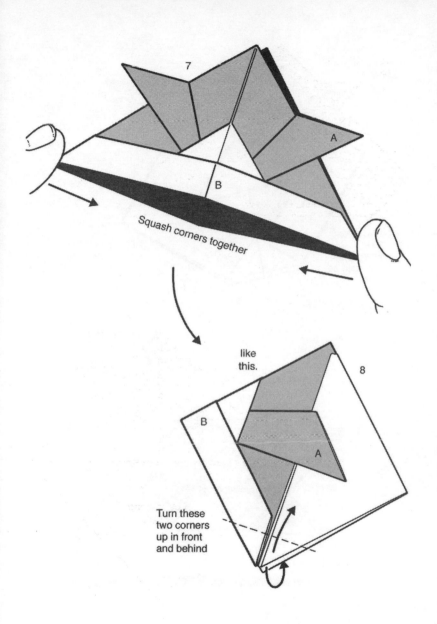

7

A

B

Squash corners together

like
this.

8

B

A

Turn these
two corners
up in front
and behind

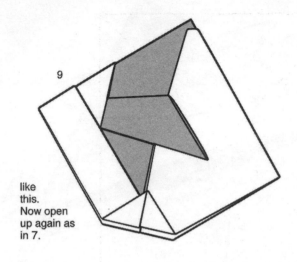

9

like
this.
Now open
up again as
in 7.

A piece of paper
50 cm (20 inches)
square will make a
hat to fit your head

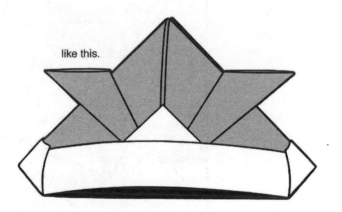

like this.

Sampan: Korean, Chinese and Japanese origin

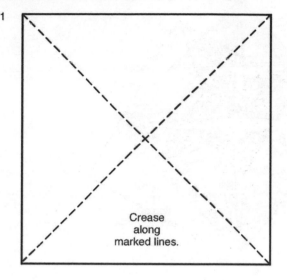

1

Crease
along
marked lines.

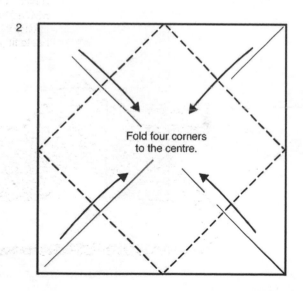

2

Fold four corners
to the centre.

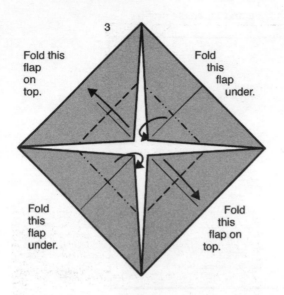

3

Fold this flap on top.

Fold this flap under.

Fold this flap under.

Fold this flap on top.

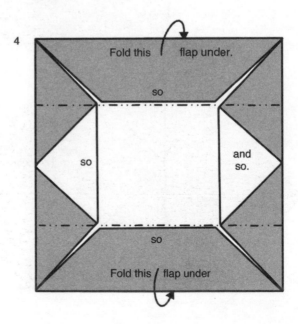

4

Fold this / flap under.

so

so

and so.

so

Fold this / flap under

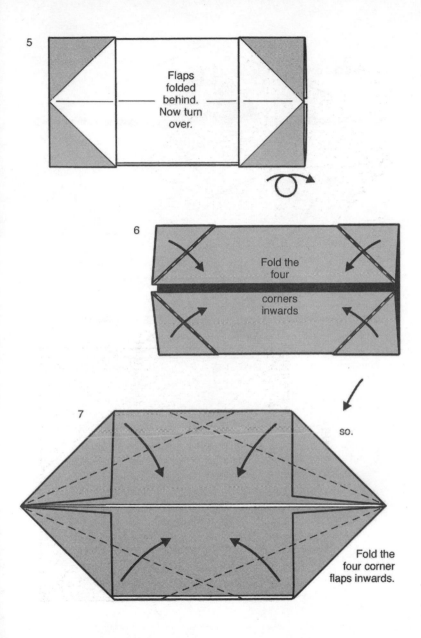

5

Flaps folded behind. Now turn over.

6

Fold the four

corners inwards

so.

7

Fold the four corner flaps inwards.

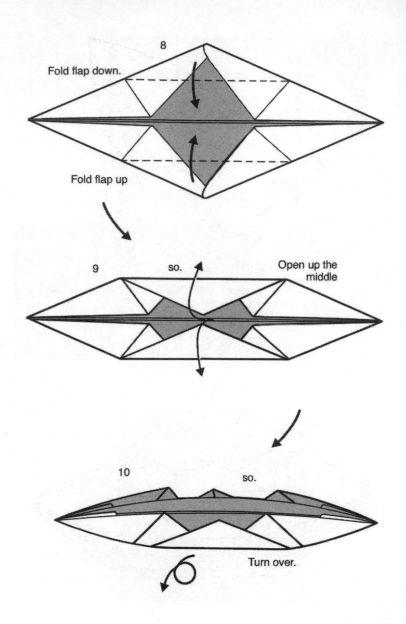

8 Fold flap down.

Fold flap up

9 so. Open up the middle

10 so. Turn over.

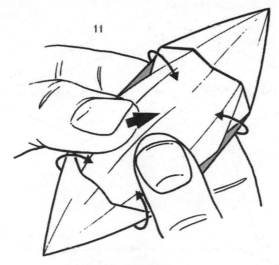

11

Press thumbs in, then
with fingers pull
sides up – and so
turn the boat
inside out. The
result will be this.

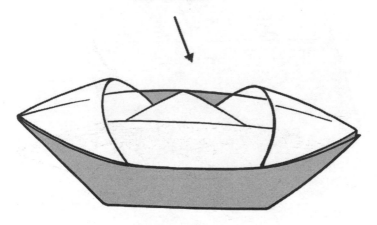

Water bomb or Japanese playball

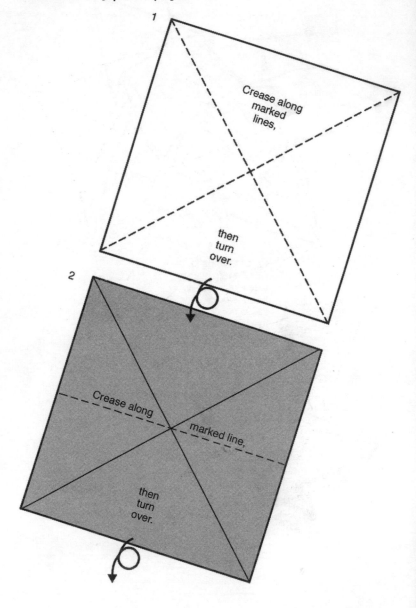

1

Crease along marked lines, then turn over.

2

Crease along marked line, then turn over.

THIS IS THE WATER BOMB BASE

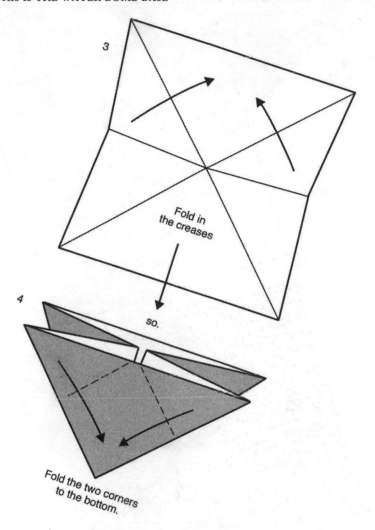

3

Fold in
the creases

so.

4

Fold the two corners
to the bottom.

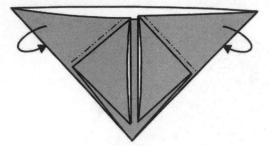

Fold the two corners behind.

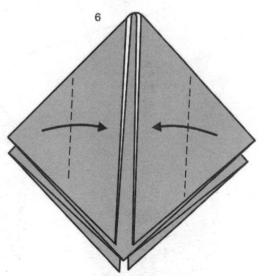

Fold the two flaps
to the centre.

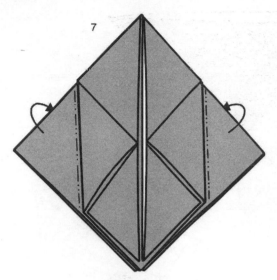

7

Fold the two
flaps behind.

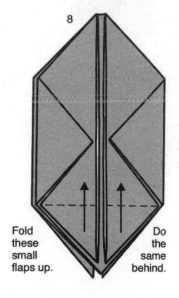

8

Fold
these
small
flaps up.

Do
the
same
behind.

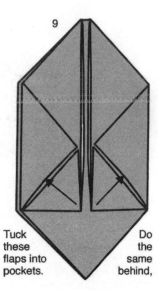

9

Tuck
these
flaps into
pockets.

Do
the
same
behind,

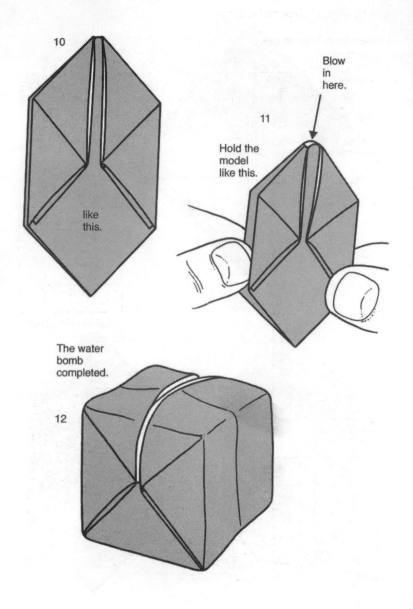

10

like
this.

Blow
in
here.

11

Hold the
model
like this.

The water
bomb
completed.

12

Cube by Shuzo Fujimoto (Japan)

Start with a 15 cm square.

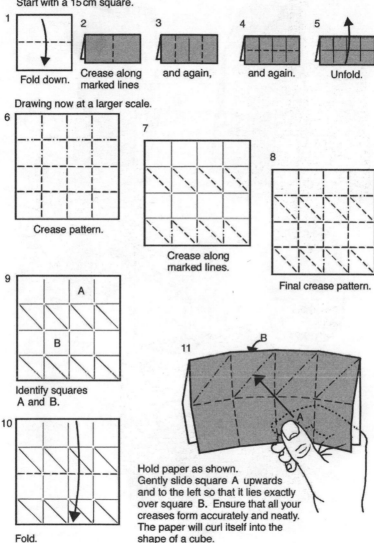

1 Fold down.

2 Crease along marked lines

3 and again,

4 and again.

5 Unfold.

Drawing now at a larger scale.

6 Crease pattern.

7 Crease along marked lines.

8 Final crease pattern.

9 Identify squares A and B.

10 Fold.

11 Hold paper as shown. Gently slide square A upwards and to the left so that it lies exactly over square B. Ensure that all your creases form accurately and neatly. The paper will curl itself into the shape of a cube.

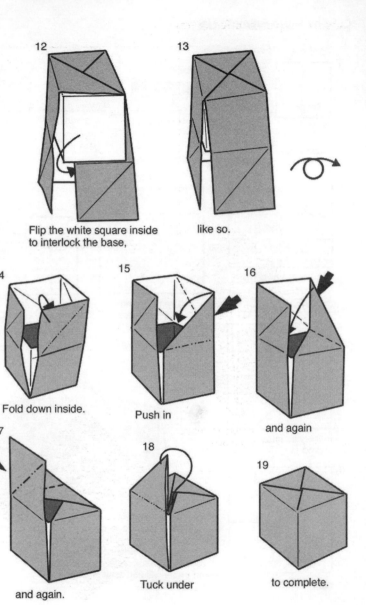

12 Flip the white square inside to interlock the base,

13 like so.

14 Fold down inside.

15 Push in

16 and again

17 and again.

18 Tuck under

19 to complete.

Sanbow 1: Japanese offering tray

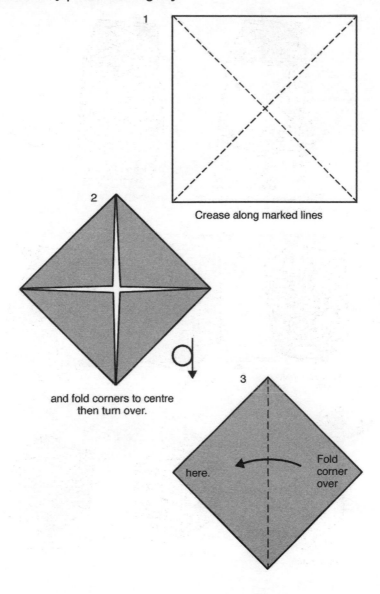

1 Crease along marked lines

2 and fold corners to centre then turn over.

3 Fold corner over here.

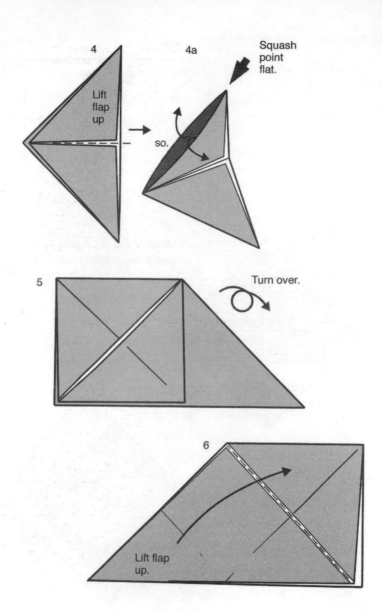

4

Lift
flap
up

so.

4a

Squash
point
flat.

5

Turn over.

6

Lift flap
up.

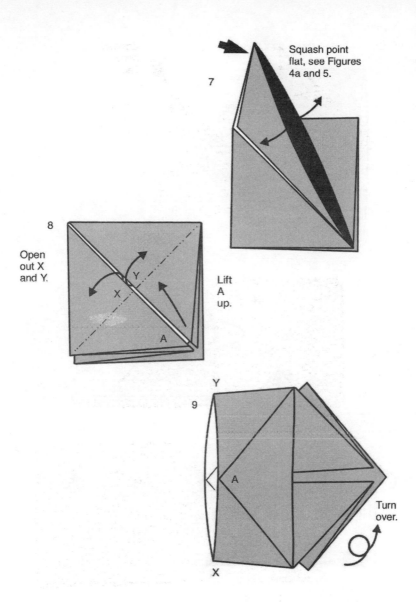

7

Squash point flat, see Figures 4a and 5.

8

Open out X and Y.

Y

X

A

Lift A up.

Y

9

A

X

Turn over.

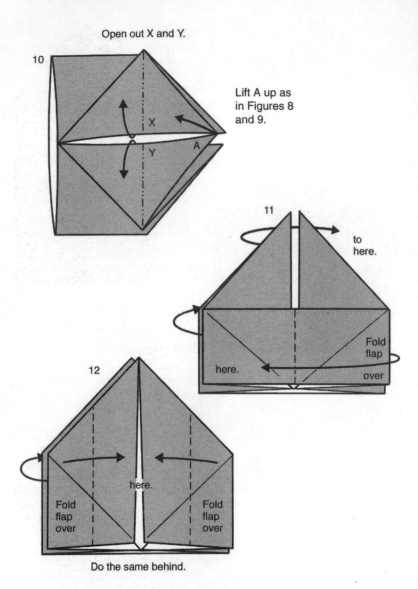

Open out X and Y.

10

X

Y

A

Lift A up as
in Figures 8
and 9.

11

to
here.

Fold
flap
over

here.

12

Fold
flap
over

here.

Fold
flap
over

Do the same behind.

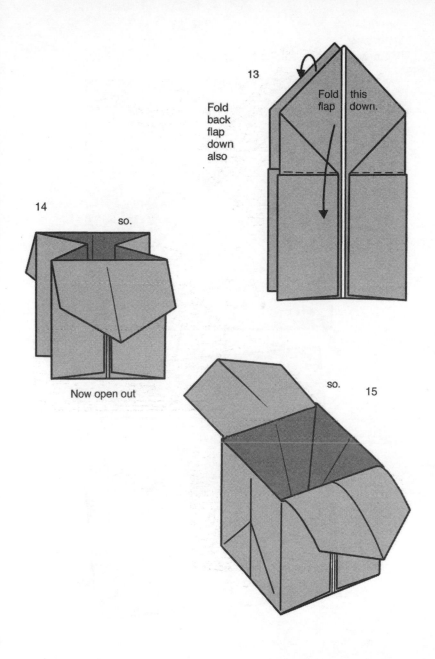

13

Fold back flap down also

Fold flap this down.

14

so.

Now open out

15

so.

Sanbow 2

Begin with corners folded to the centre.

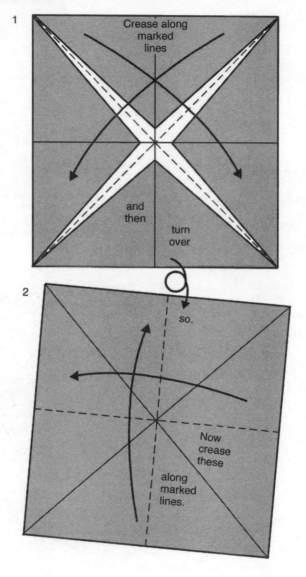

1

Crease along marked lines

and then

turn over

so.

2

Now crease these

along marked lines.

Japanese offering tray, different method

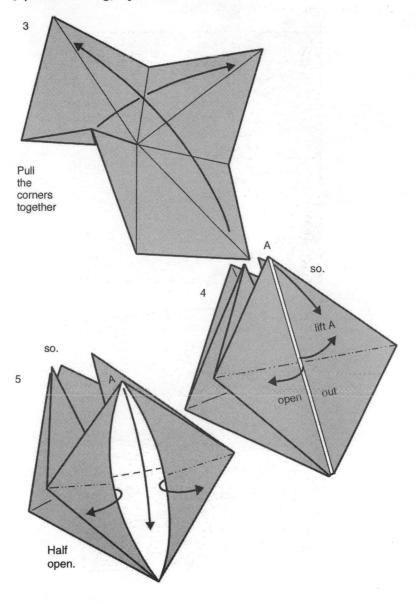

3

Pull
the
corners
together

A

so.

4

lift A

open   out

so.

5

A

Half
open.

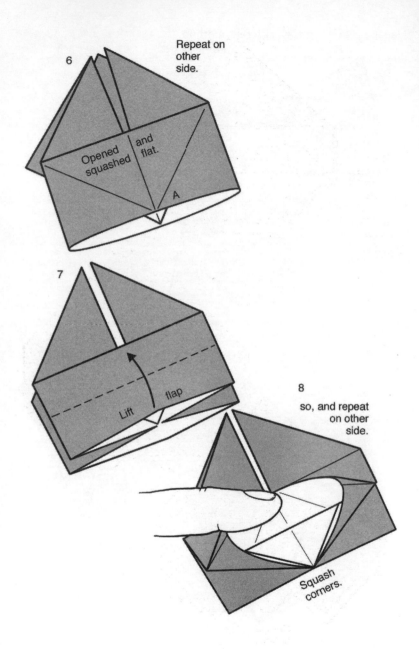

6

Repeat on other side.

Opened squashed and flat.

A

7

Lift

flap

8

so, and repeat on other side.

Squash corners.

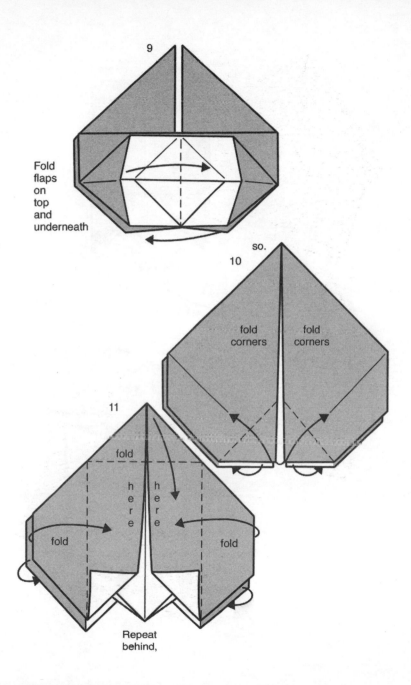

9

Fold
flaps
on
top
and
underneath

so.

10

fold
corners

fold
corners

11

fold

h
e
r
e

h
e
r
e

fold

fold

Repeat
behind,

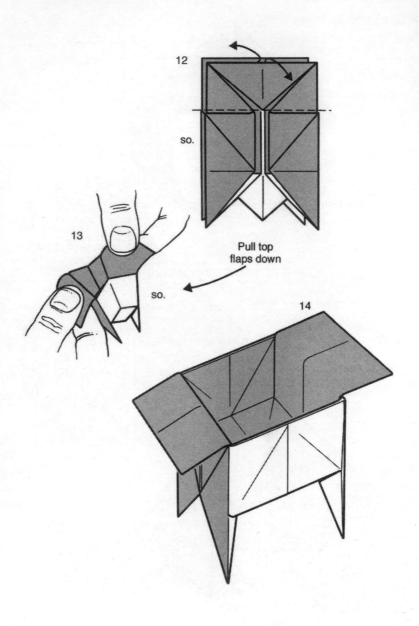

12

so.

Pull top
flaps down

13

so.

14

Dish by Philip Shen (Hong Kong)

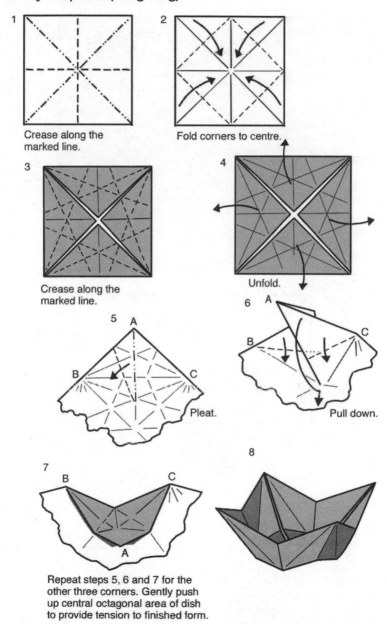

1 Crease along the marked line.

2 Fold corners to centre.

3 Crease along the marked line.

4 Unfold.

5 Pleat.

6 Pull down.

7 Repeat steps 5, 6 and 7 for the other three corners. Gently push up central octagonal area of dish to provide tension to finished form.

8

Basket or Japanese box with handle

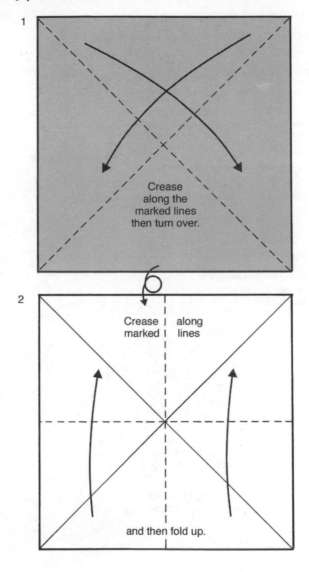

1

Crease along the marked lines then turn over.

2

Crease along marked lines

and then fold up.

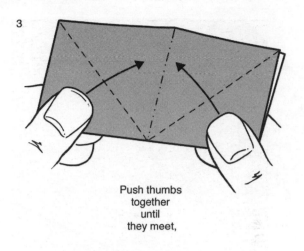

3

Push thumbs
together
until
they meet,

so.

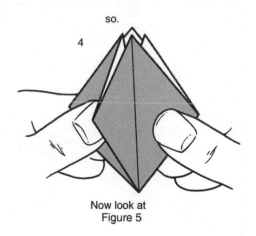

4

Now look at
Figure 5

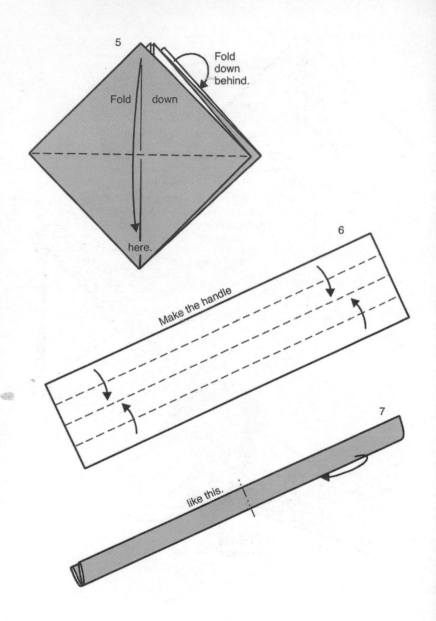

5 Fold down behind.

Fold down here.

6 Make the handle

7 like this.

78

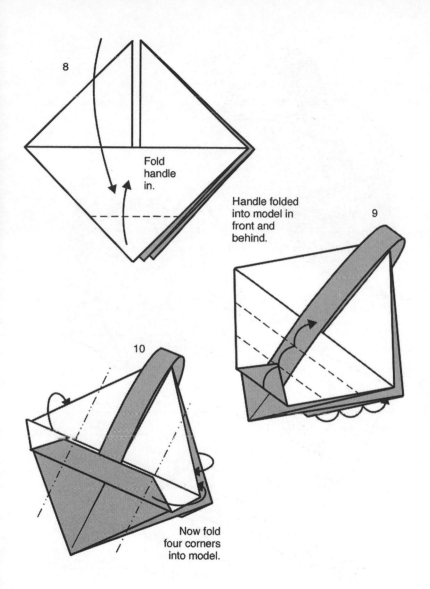

8

Fold
handle
in.

Handle folded
into model in
front and
behind.

9

10

Now fold
four corners
into model.

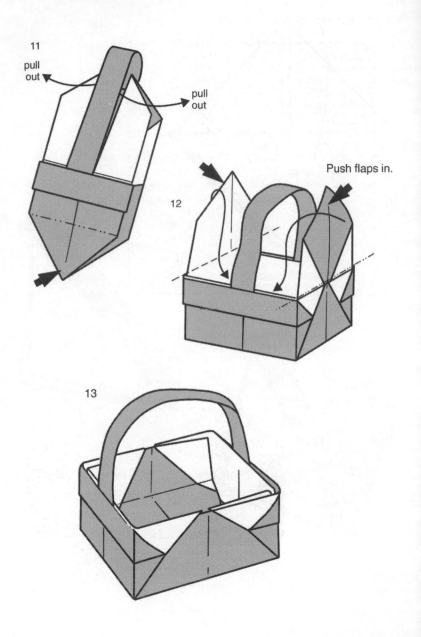

11

pull
out

pull
out

12

Push flaps in.

13

Multiform: series of standard folds

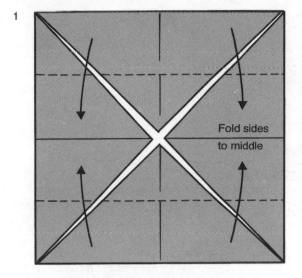

1

Fold sides
to middle

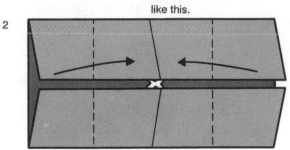

2

like this.

Fold sides to the middle.

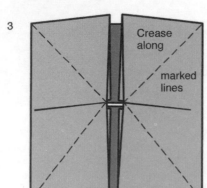

3

Crease
along

marked
lines

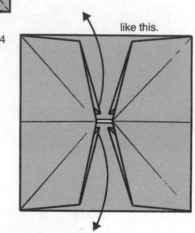

like this.

4

Now pull out the
two arrowed
points. The creases
will guide you and
they will fall into
place as in Figure 5,

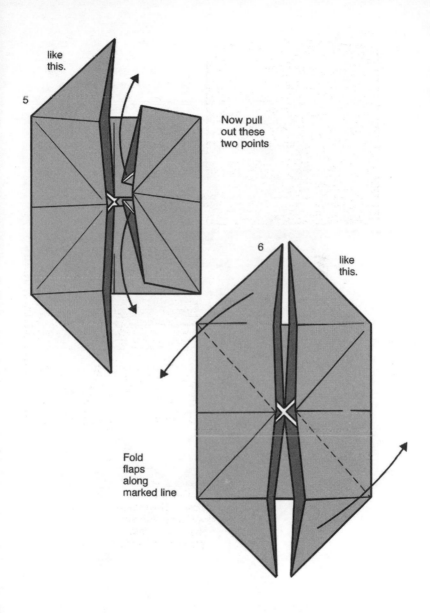

like
this.

5

Now pull
out these
two points

6

like
this.

Fold
flaps
along
marked line

Windmill and vase

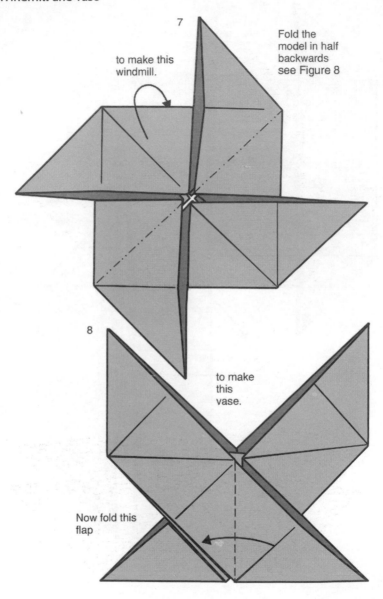

7

to make this
windmill.

Fold the
model in half
backwards
see Figure 8

8

to make
this
vase.

Now fold this
flap

Sailboat and catamaran

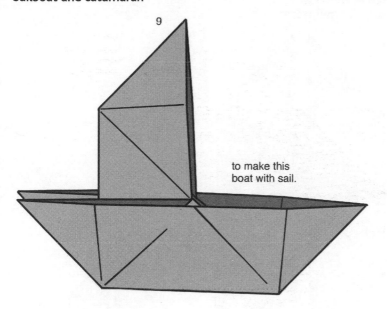

9

to make this
boat with sail.

Now start at Figure 6
and fold the model in
half to make this
catamaran.

10

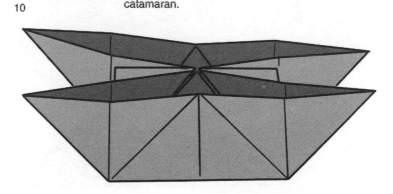

Gondola
Begin with multiform fold 6.

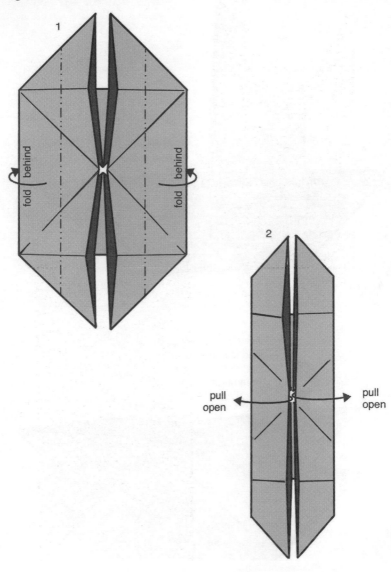

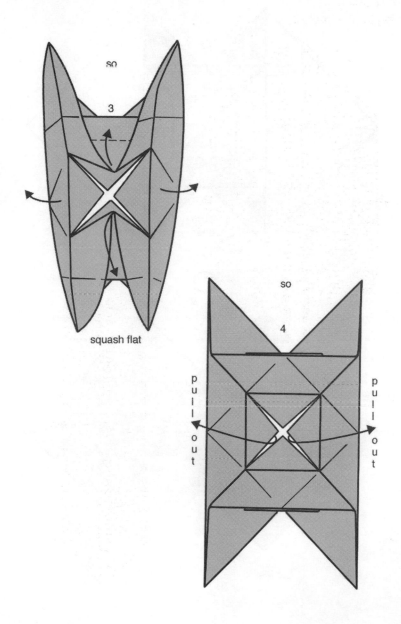

squash flat

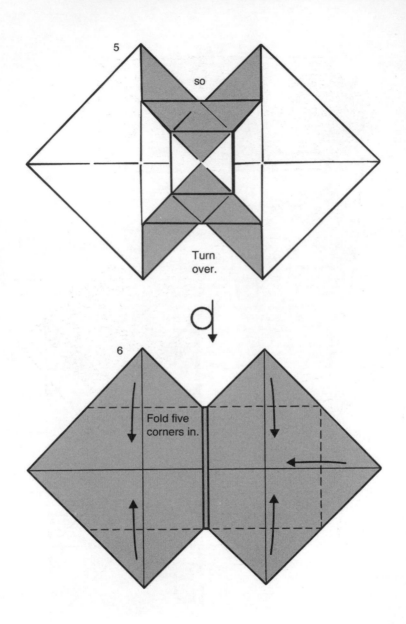

5

so

Turn
over.

6

Fold five
corners in.

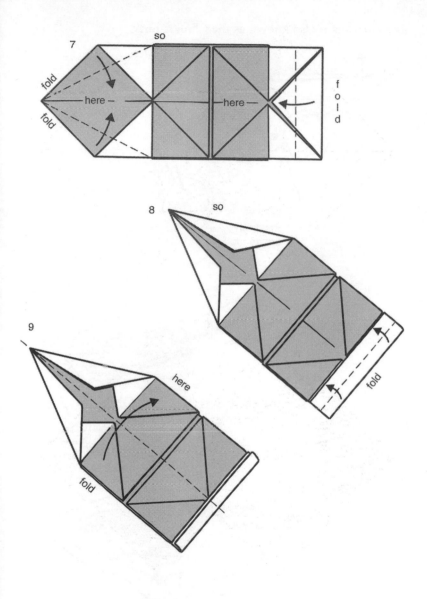

The Gondola is also known as the Chinese junk.

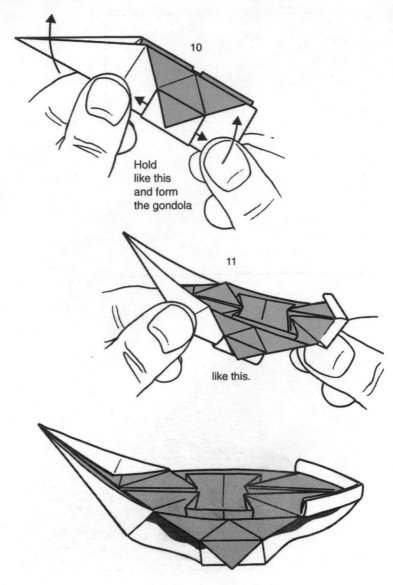

10

Hold
like this
and form
the gondola

11

like this.

Bird base: the most important base in origami

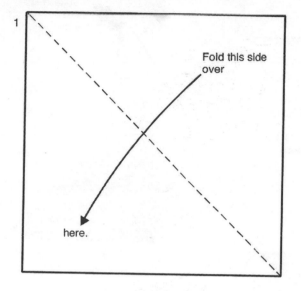

Fold this side over

here.

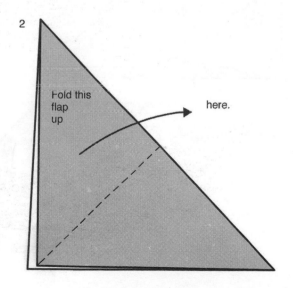

Fold this flap up

here.

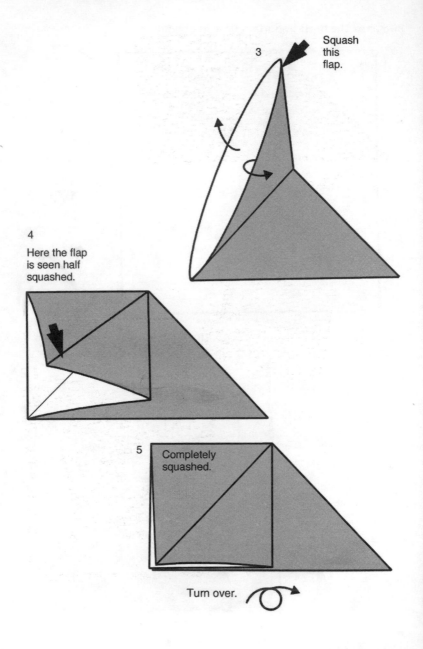

3 Squash this flap.

4 Here the flap is seen half squashed.

5 Completely squashed.

Turn over.

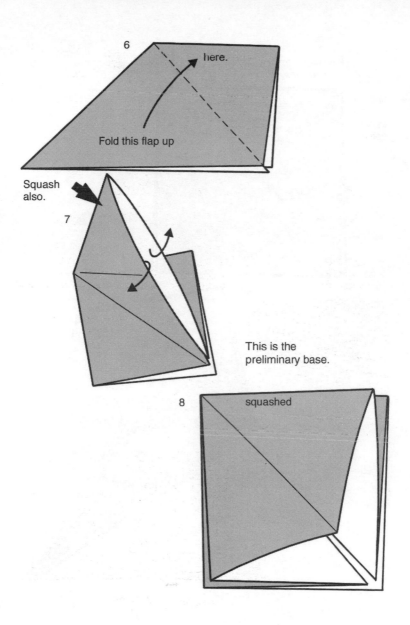

6

here.

Fold this flap up

Squash also.

7

This is the preliminary base.

8   squashed

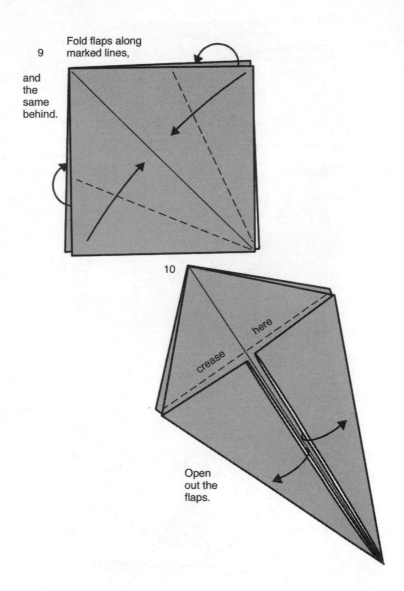

9 Fold flaps along marked lines,

and the same behind.

10 crease here

Open out the flaps.

94

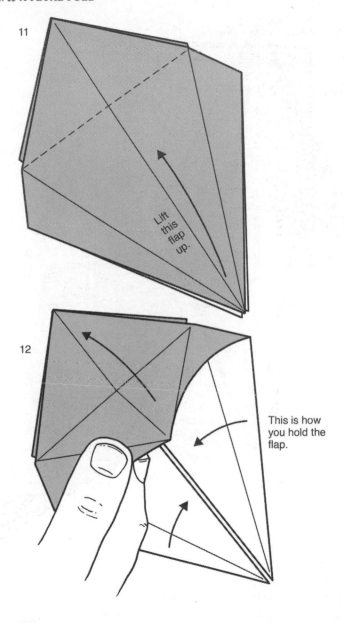

11

Lift
this
flap
up.

12

This is how
you hold the
flap.

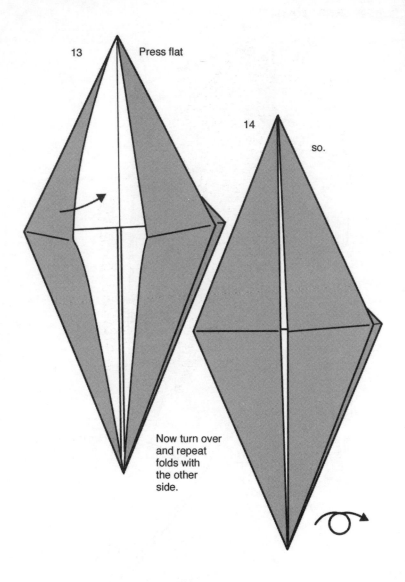

13 Press flat

14 so.

Now turn over
and repeat
folds with
the other
side.

THIS IS THE BIRD BASE

15

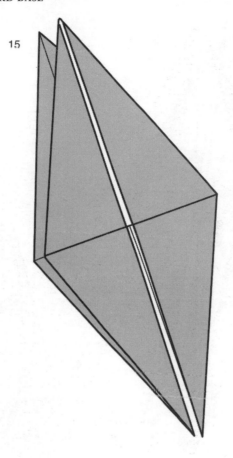

Flapping bird: ancient Japanese

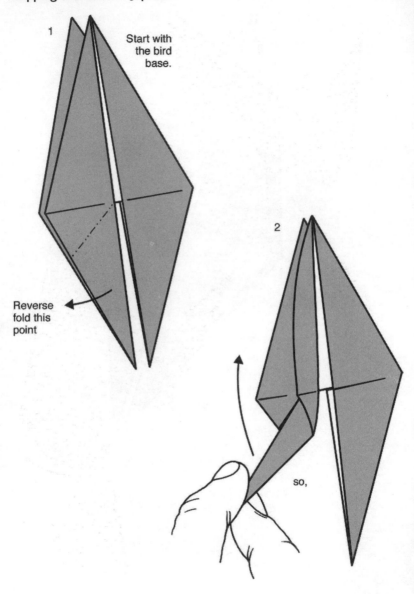

1

Start with the bird base.

Reverse fold this point

2

so,

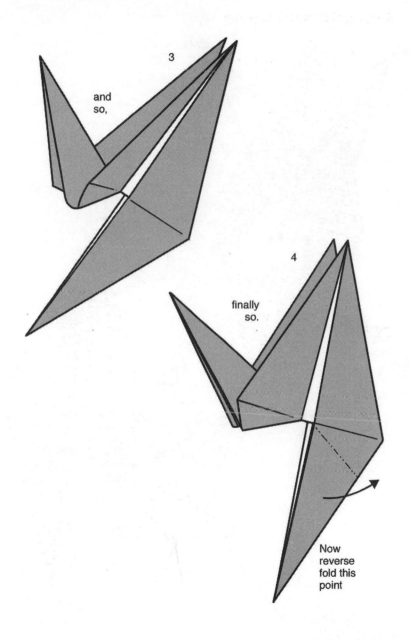

3

and
so,

4

finally
so.

Now
reverse
fold this
point

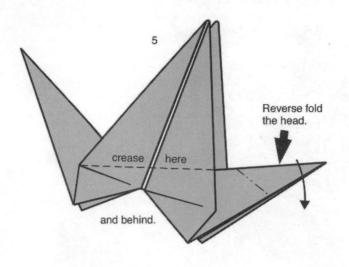

5

Reverse fold
the head.

crease here

and behind.

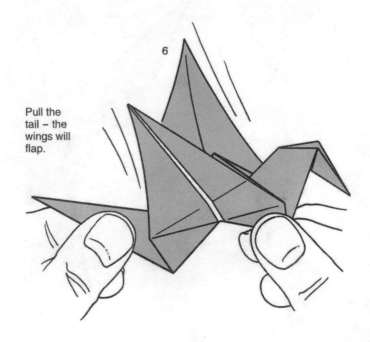

6

Pull the
tail – the
wings will
flap.

Pigeon by Akira Yoshizawa (Tokyo, Japan)

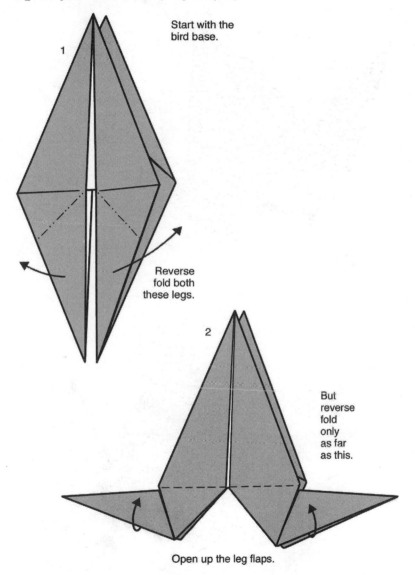

Start with the bird base.

1

Reverse fold both these legs.

2

But reverse fold only as far as this.

Open up the leg flaps.

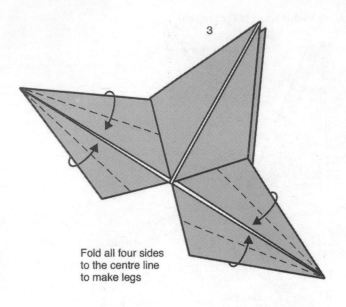

3

Fold all four sides
to the centre line
to make legs

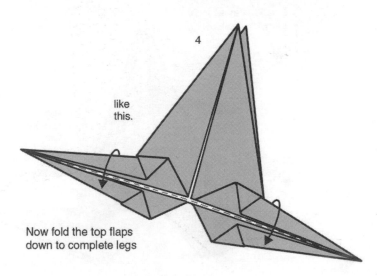

4

like
this.

Now fold the top flaps
down to complete legs

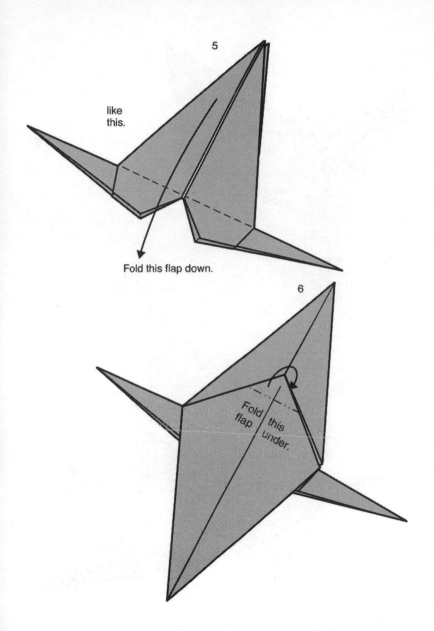

5

like
this.

Fold this flap down.

6

Fold this
flap under.

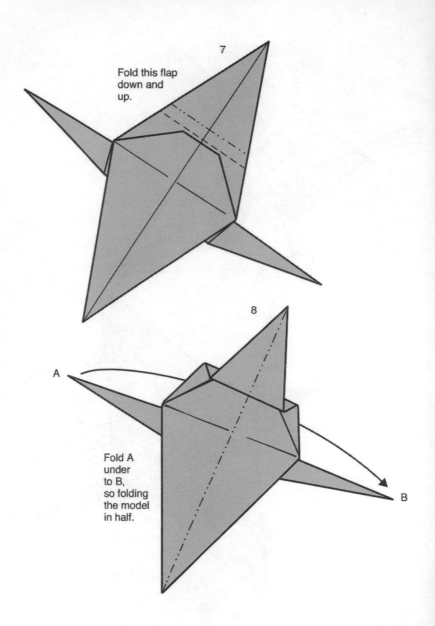

7

Fold this flap down and up.

8

Fold A under to B, so folding the model in half.

A

B

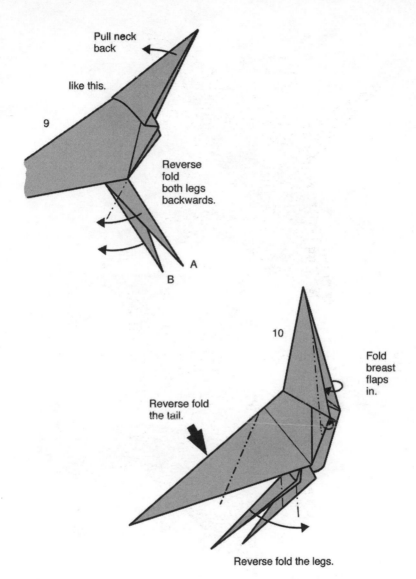

Pull neck back

like this.

9

Reverse fold both legs backwards.

A

B

10

Fold breast flaps in.

Reverse fold the tail.

Reverse fold the legs.

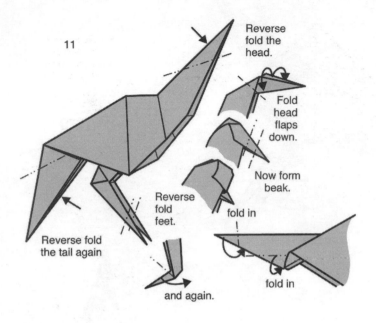

11

Reverse fold the head.

Fold head flaps down.

Now form beak.

fold in

fold in

Reverse fold feet.

Reverse fold the tail again

and again.

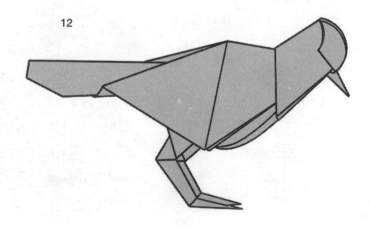

12

Praying moor: Spanish origin
Start with bird base.

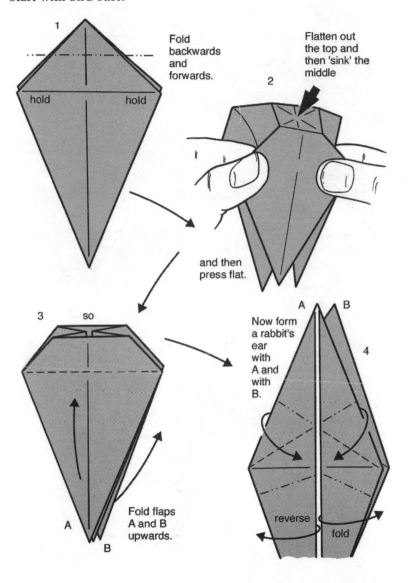

1

Fold backwards and forwards.

hold   hold

Flatten out the top and then 'sink' the middle

2

and then press flat.

3   so

Fold flaps A and B upwards.

A

B

Now form a rabbit's ear with A and with B.

A   B

4

reverse   fold

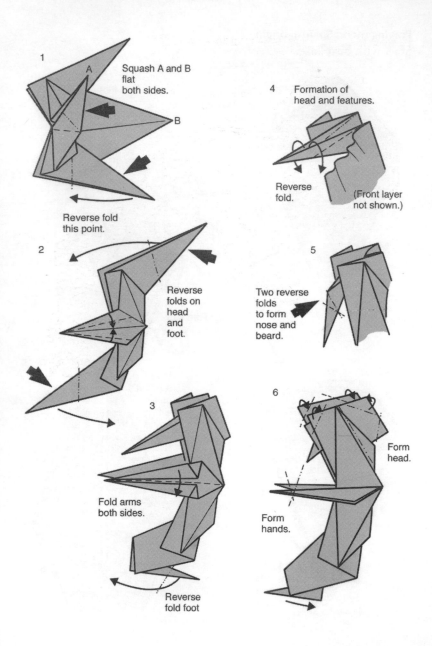

1 Squash A and B flat both sides.

Reverse fold this point.

2 Reverse folds on head and foot.

3 Fold arms both sides.

Reverse fold foot

4 Formation of head and features.

Reverse fold.

(Front layer not shown.)

5 Two reverse folds to form nose and beard.

6 Form head.

Form hands.

The praying moor completed.

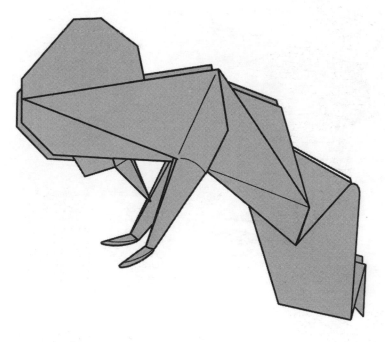

Frog
Start with preliminary base.

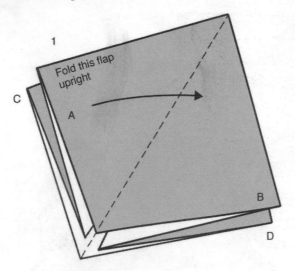

1

Fold this flap upright

C

A

B

D

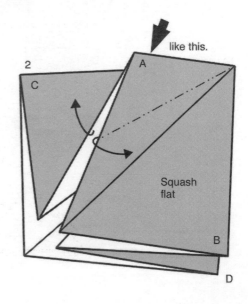

like this.

2

C

A

Squash flat

B

D

THIS IS A SQUASH FOLD

3

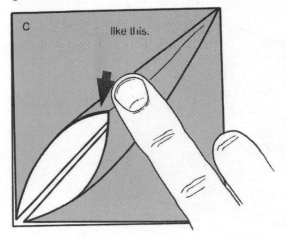

C

like this.

4

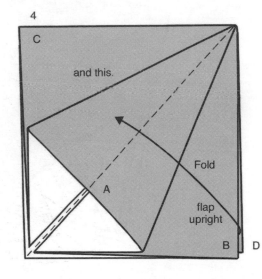

C

and this.

Fold

flap
upright

A

B   D

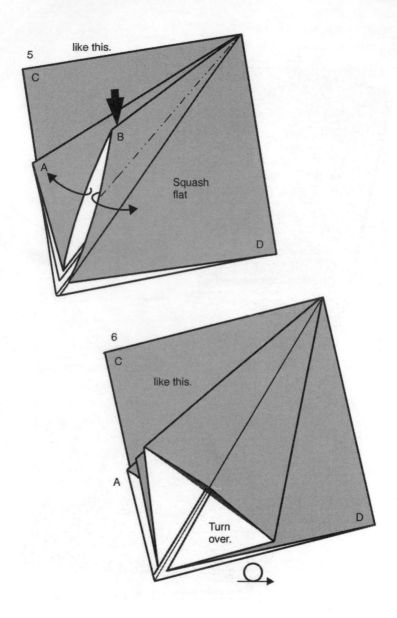

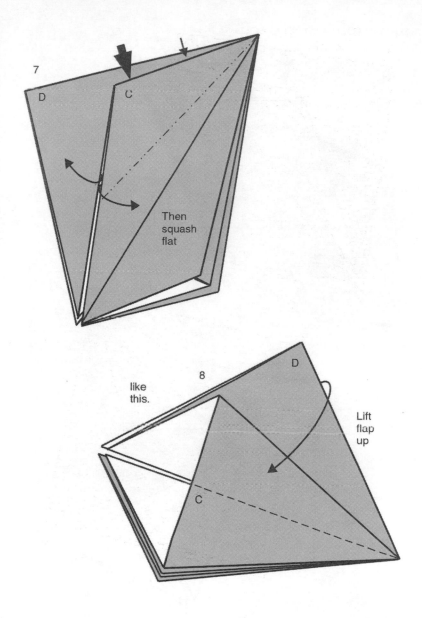

7

D

C

Then
squash
flat

like
this.

8

D

Lift
flap
up

C

SQUASH FOLD AND PETAL FOLD

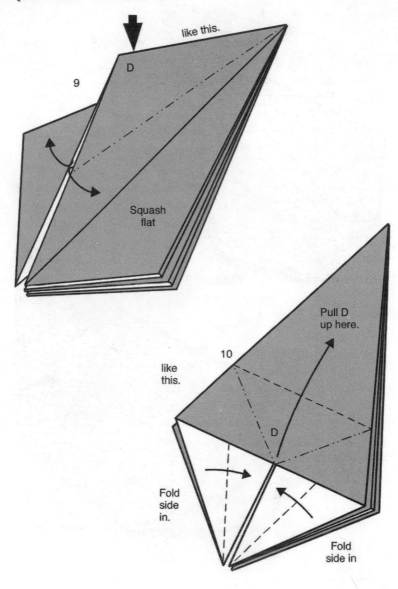

like this.

9

D

Squash
flat

Pull D
up here.

like
this.

10

D

Fold
side
in.

Fold
side in

PETAL FOLD COMPLETED

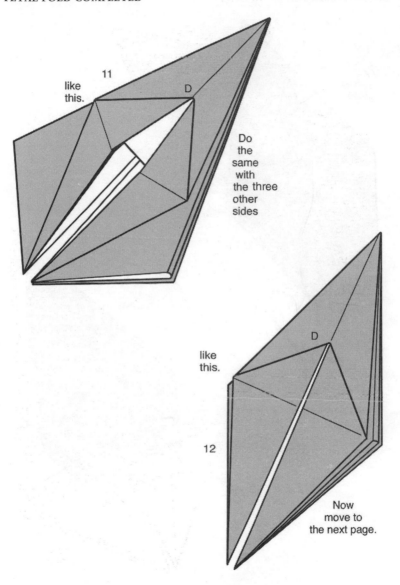

like
this.

11

D

Do
the
same
with
the three
other
sides

like
this.

D

12

Now
move to
the next page.

THIS IS THE FROG BASE

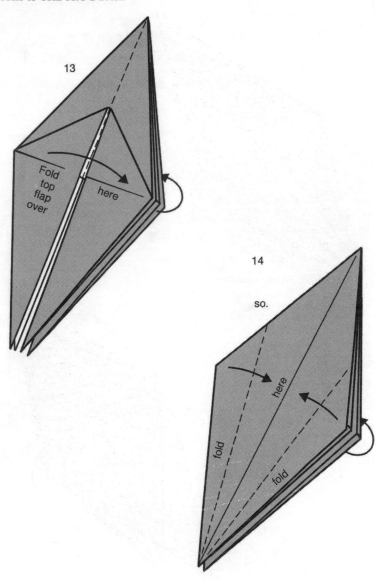

13

Fold
top
flap
over

here

14

so.

here

fold

fold

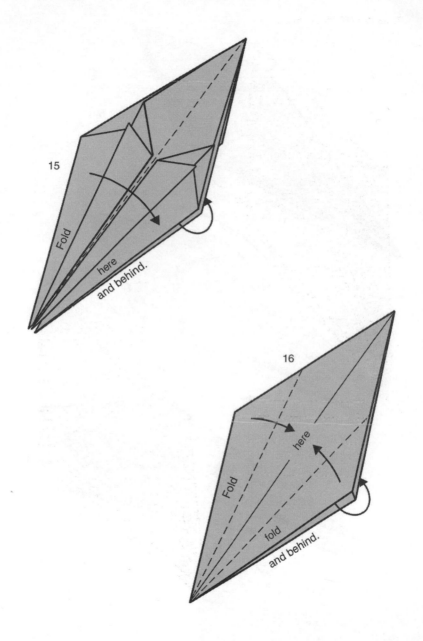

15

Fold

here

and behind.

16

Fold

here

fold

and behind.

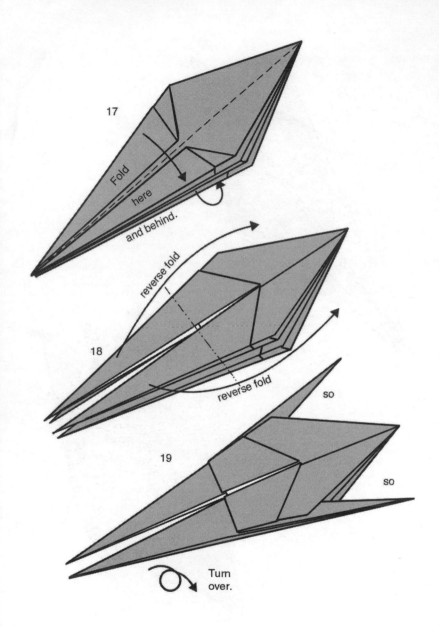

17 Fold here and behind.

18 reverse fold
reverse fold

19 so
so

Turn over.

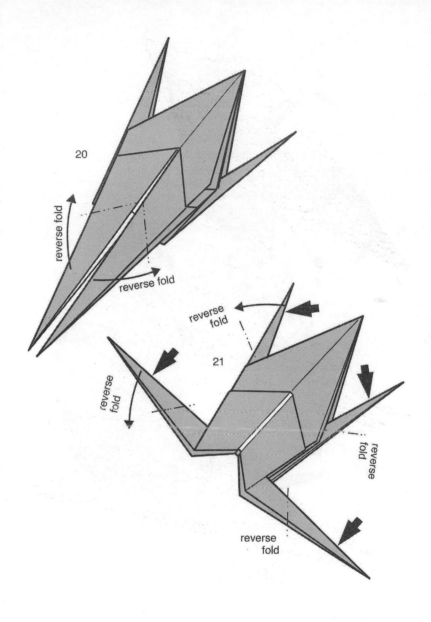

20

reverse fold

reverse fold

reverse fold

21

reverse fold

reverse fold

reverse fold

reverse fold

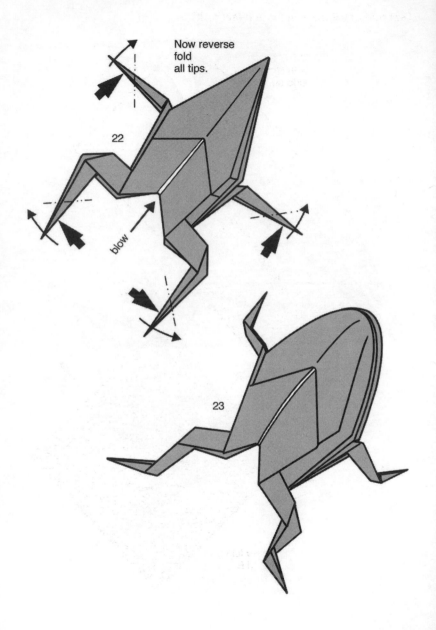

Now reverse
fold
all tips.

22

blow

23

Bat mask by Peter Van Note (New York)

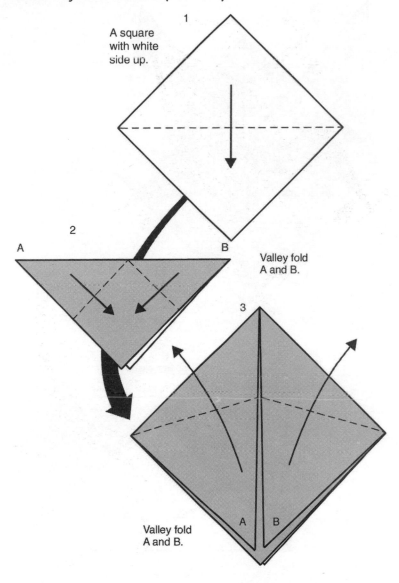

1

A square with white side up.

2

A

B

Valley fold A and B.

3

Valley fold A and B.

A B

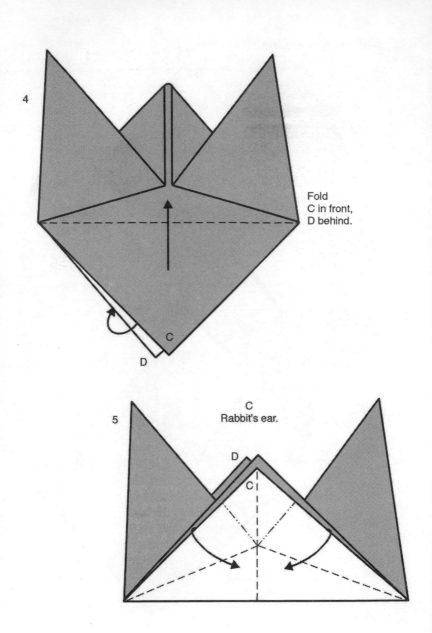

4

Fold
C in front,
D behind.

D

C

5

C
Rabbit's ear.

D

C

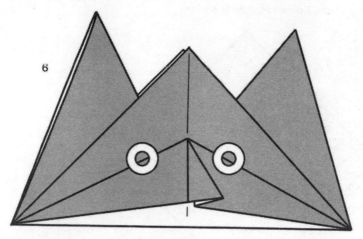

6

Make eyes with gummed eyelets.

Penguins by Robert Harbin (London)

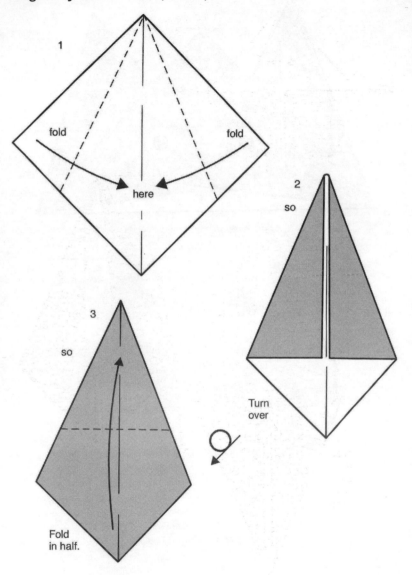

1

fold   fold

here

2

so

Turn
over

3

so

Fold
in half.

THIS IS THE FISH BASE

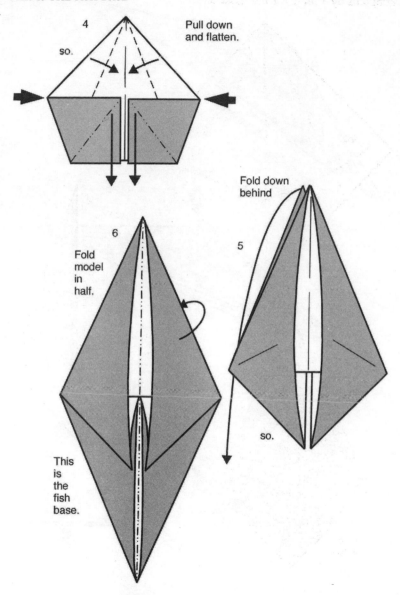

4

so.

Pull down and flatten.

Fold down behind

5

so.

6

Fold model in half.

This is the fish base.

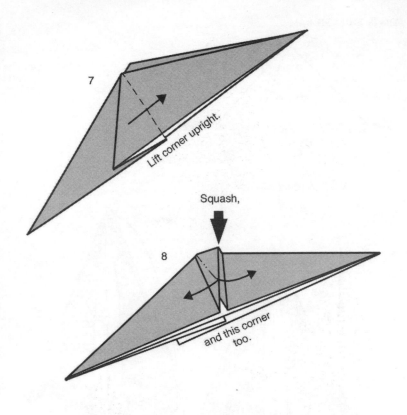

7

Lift corner upright.

Squash,

8

and this corner too.

Reverse fold both points

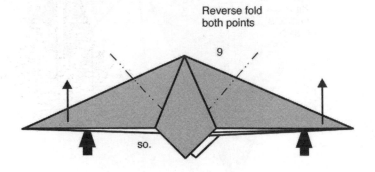

9

so.

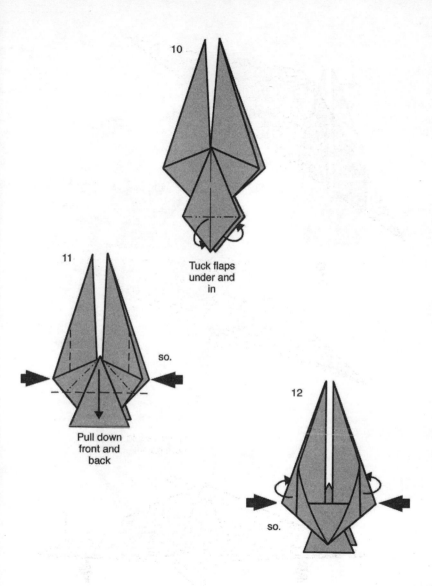

10

Tuck flaps
under and
in

11

so.

Pull down
front and
back

12

so.

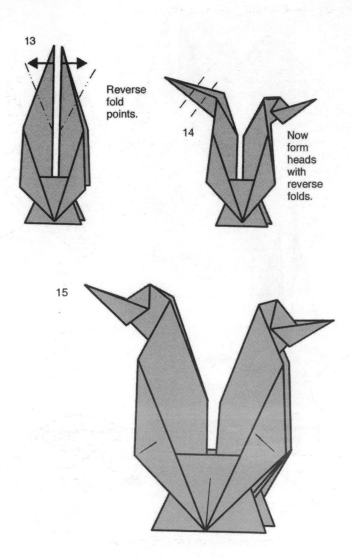

13 Reverse fold points.

14 Now form heads with reverse folds.

15

Penguin 1 by Eric Bird (Leicester, England)

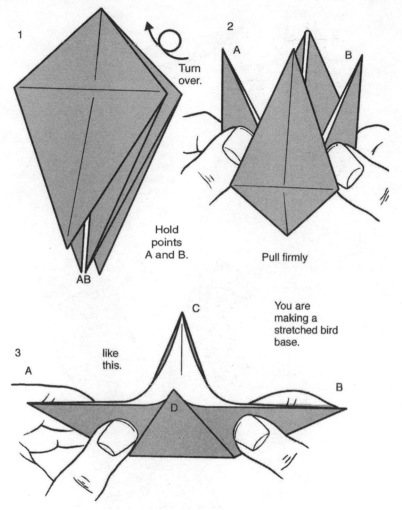

1

Turn over.

Hold points A and B.

2

A B

Pull firmly

AB

3

A

like this.

C

You are making a stretched bird base.

D

B

Bring C and D together and press flat.

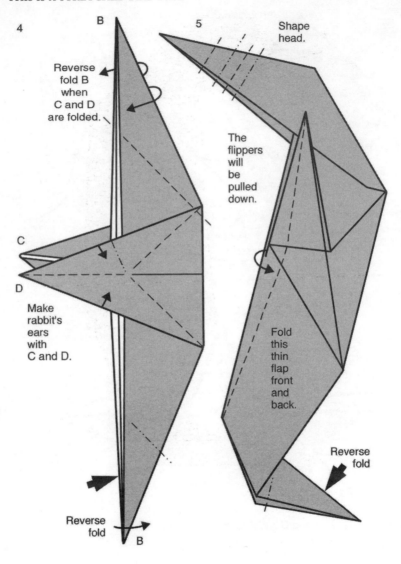

4

B

Reverse
fold B
when
C and D
are folded.

C

D

Make
rabbit's
ears
with
C and D.

Reverse
fold

B

5

Shape
head.

The
flippers
will
be
pulled
down.

Fold
this
thin
flap
front
and
back.

Reverse
fold

6

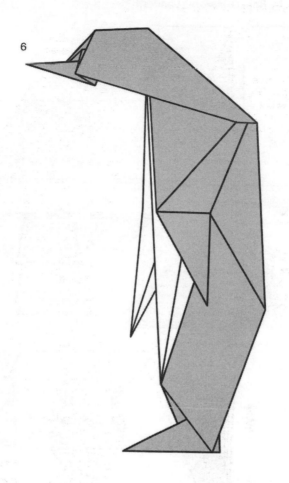

Penguin 2 by Robert Harbin (London)

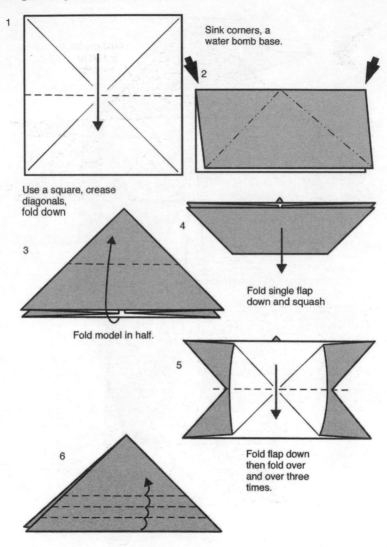

1 Use a square, crease diagonals, fold down

Sink corners, a water bomb base.

2

3 Fold model in half.

4 Fold single flap down and squash

5 Fold flap down then fold over and over three times.

6

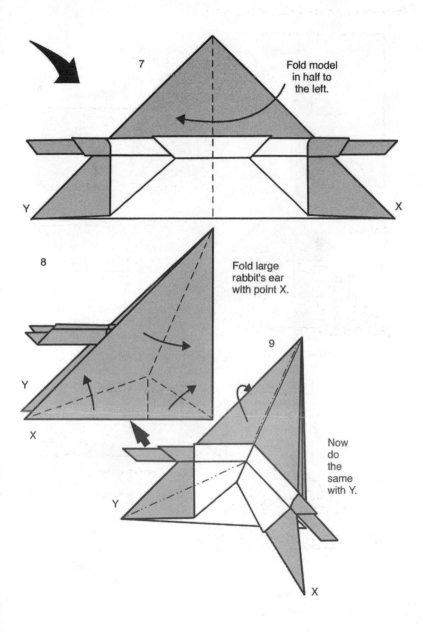

7

Fold model in half to the left.

Y

X

8

Fold large rabbit's ear with point X.

Y

X

9

Now do the same with Y.

Y

X

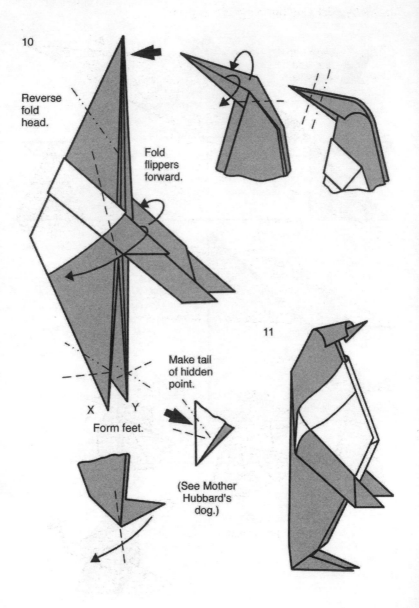

10

Reverse fold head.

Fold flippers forward.

Make tail of hidden point.

X   Y

Form feet.

(See Mother Hubbard's dog.)

11

Rabbit by Mick Guy (Birmingham, England)

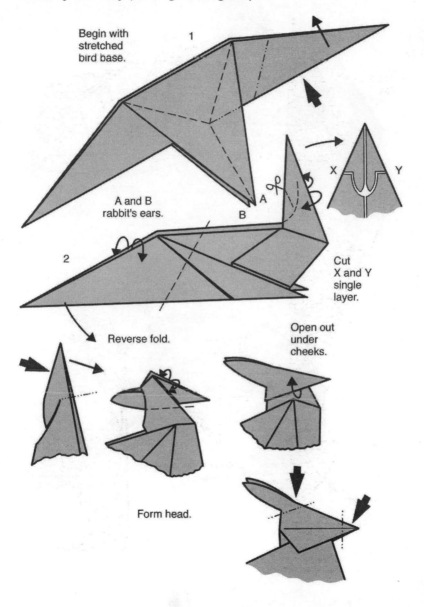

Begin with stretched bird base.

1

A and B rabbit's ears.

X   Y

Cut X and Y single layer.

2

Reverse fold.

Open out under cheeks.

Form head.

Using the stretched bird base (see Penguin 1).

3

4 Round body off.

5

Tropical bird 1 by Ligia Montoya (Argentina)
Use the Fish base (see Penguins).

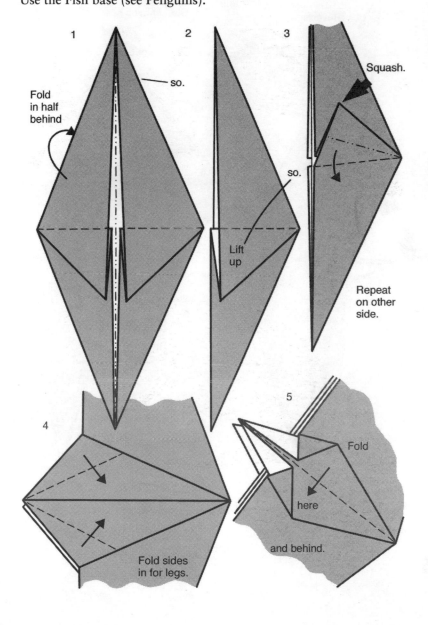

1

so.

Fold
in half
behind

2

so.

Lift
up

3

Squash.

Repeat
on other
side.

4

Fold sides
in for legs.

5

Fold

here

and behind.

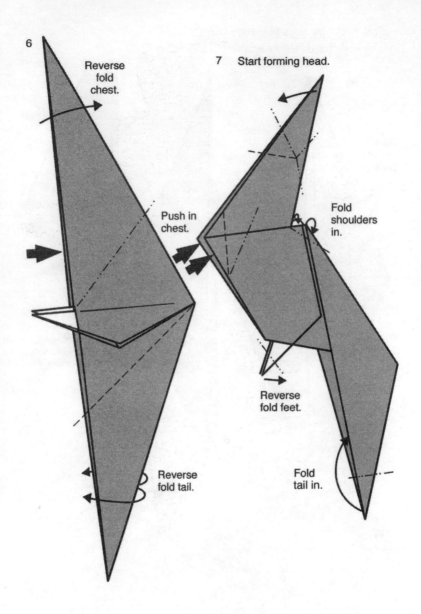

6

Reverse
fold
chest.

7 Start forming head.

Push in
chest.

Fold
shoulders
in.

Reverse
fold feet.

Reverse
fold tail.

Fold
tail in.

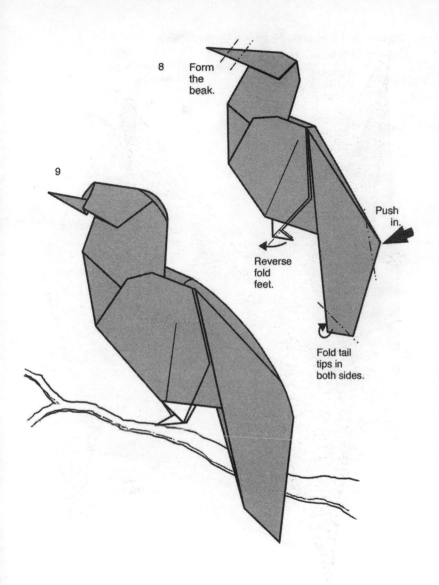

8 Form the beak.

9

Push in.

Reverse fold feet.

Fold tail tips in both sides.

Tropical bird 2 by Ligia Montoya (Argentina)
Use the Fish base again.

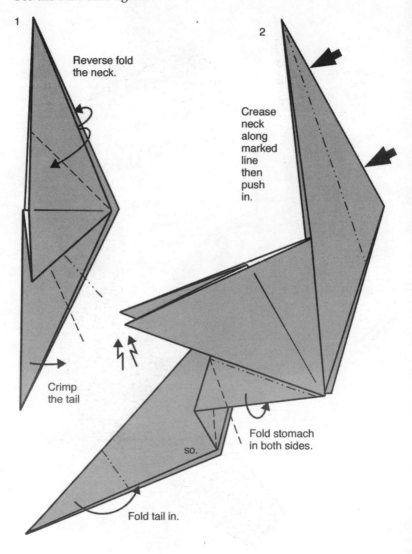

1

Reverse fold
the neck.

2

Crease
neck
along
marked
line
then
push
in.

Crimp
the tail

Fold stomach
in both sides.

so.

Fold tail in.

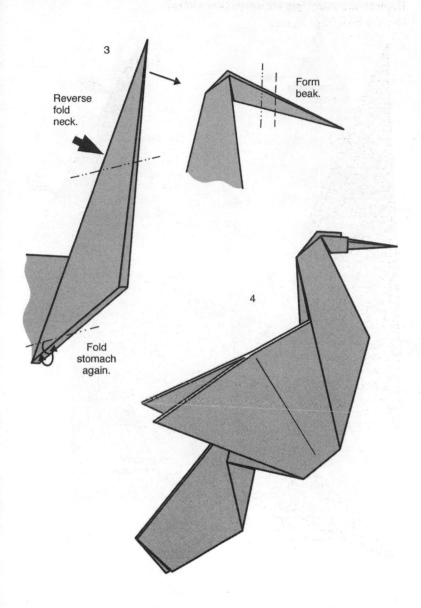

3

Reverse
fold
neck.

Form
beak.

Fold
stomach
again.

4

Christmas tree by Robert Harbin (London)

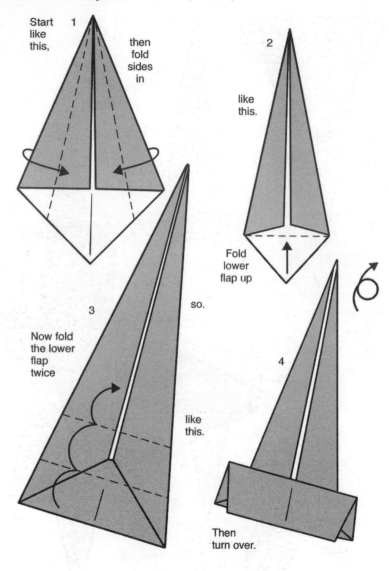

Start like this, then fold sides in

1

2

like this.

Fold lower flap up

3

so.

Now fold the lower flap twice

like this.

4

Then turn over.

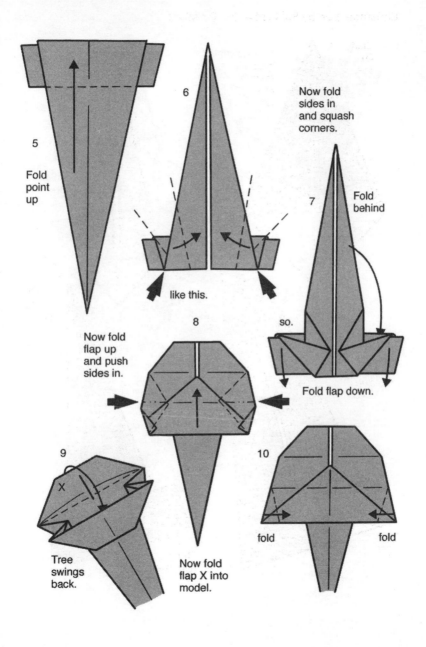

5 Fold point up

6

Now fold sides in and squash corners.

7 Fold behind

like this.

so.

Fold flap down.

Now fold flap up and push sides in.

8

Now fold flap X into model.

9

X

Tree swings back.

10

fold   fold

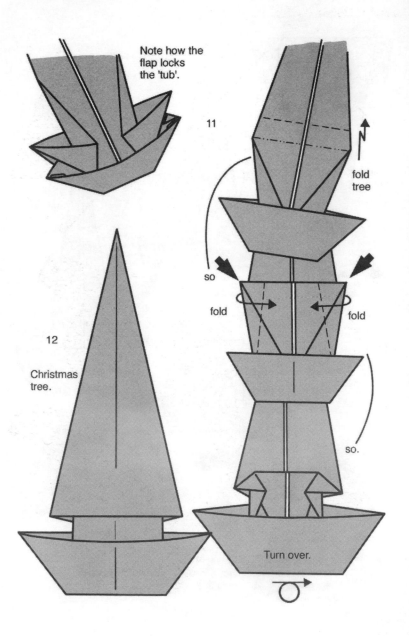

Note how the flap locks the 'tub'.

11

fold tree

so

fold   fold

12

Christmas tree.

so.

Turn over.

Mother Hubbard's dog

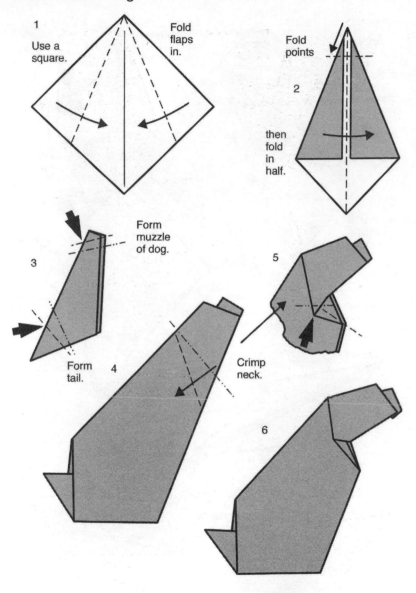

1 Use a square. Fold flaps in.

2 Fold points then fold in half.

3 Form muzzle of dog. Form tail.

4 Crimp neck.

5

6

Mother Hubbard by Eric Kenneway (London)

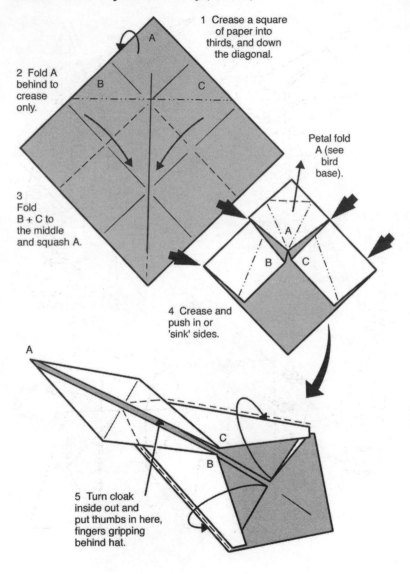

1 Crease a square of paper into thirds, and down the diagonal.

2 Fold A behind to crease only.

3 Fold B + C to the middle and squash A.

Petal fold A (see bird base).

4 Crease and push in or 'sink' sides.

5 Turn cloak inside out and put thumbs in here, fingers gripping behind hat.

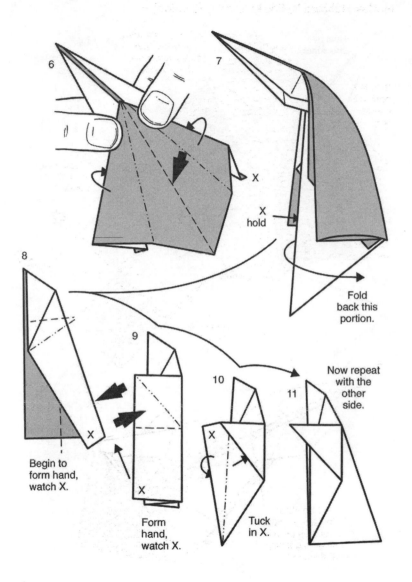

6

7

X

X
hold

Fold
back this
portion.

8

9

Now repeat
with the
other
side.

10

11

Begin to
form hand,
watch X.

X

Form
hand,
watch X.

X

X

Tuck
in X.

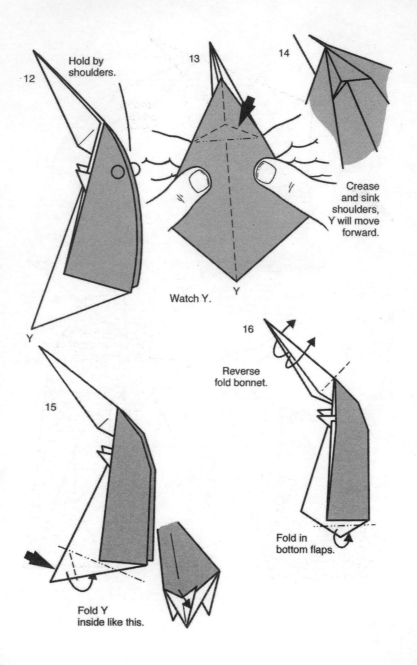

12

Hold by shoulders.

13

Watch Y.

Y

Y

14

Crease and sink shoulders, Y will move forward.

15

Fold Y inside like this.

16

Reverse fold bonnet.

Fold in bottom flaps.

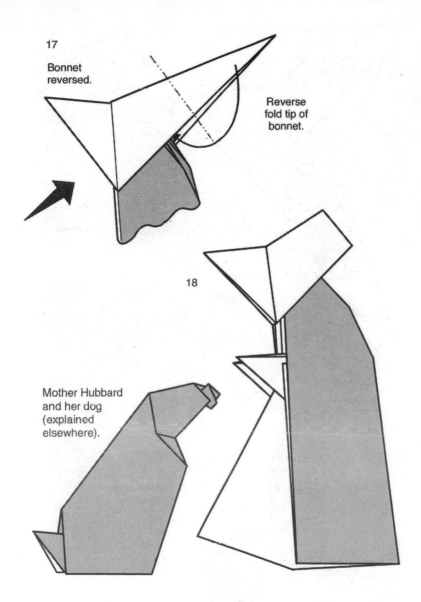

17

Bonnet reversed.

Reverse fold tip of bonnet.

18

Mother Hubbard and her dog (explained elsewhere).

Friar Tuck by Eric Kenneway (London)

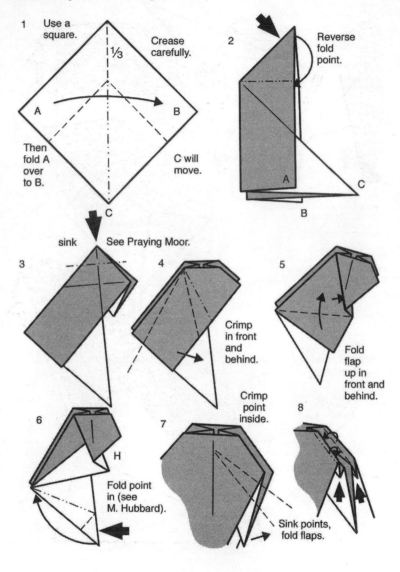

1 Use a square. Crease carefully.

⅓

A → B

Then fold A over to B.

C will move.

C

2 Reverse fold point.

A

C

B

sink   See Praying Moor.

3

4 Crimp in front and behind.

5 Fold flap up in front and behind.

6 Fold point in (see M. Hubbard).

H

Crimp point inside.

7 Sink points, fold flaps.

8

Friar Tuck carrying Robin Hood

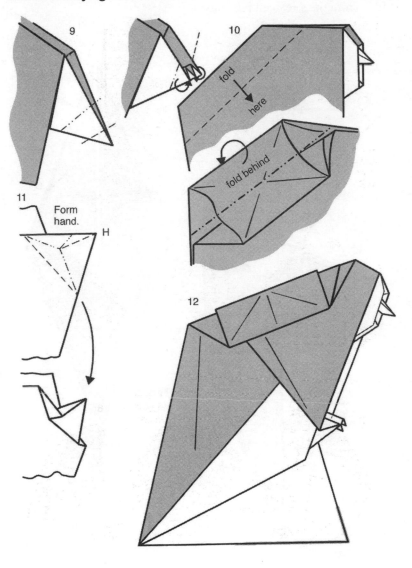

Squirrel by Merton H. Wolfman (Liverpool, England)
Made from the stretched bird base.

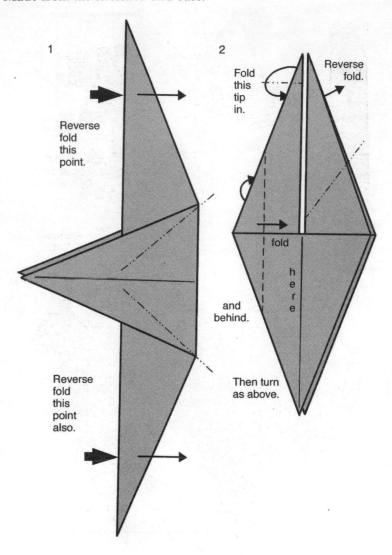

1

Reverse fold this point.

Reverse fold this point also.

2

Fold this tip in.

Reverse fold.

fold

here

and behind.

Then turn as above.

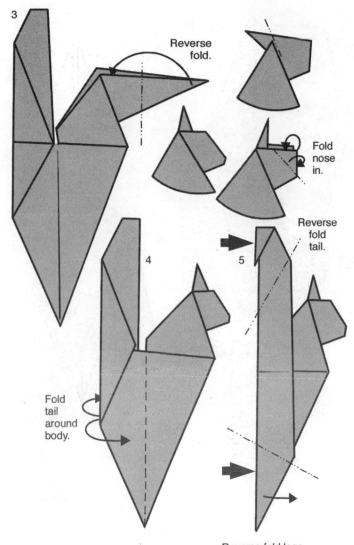

3

Reverse
fold.

Fold
nose
in.

Reverse
fold
tail.

4

5

Fold
tail
around
body.

Reverse fold legs.

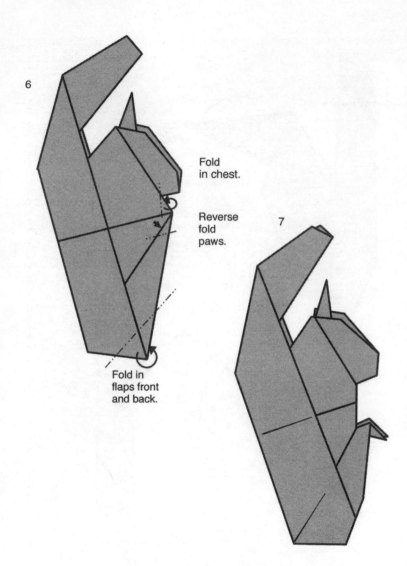

6

Fold
in chest.

Reverse
fold
paws.

7

Fold in
flaps front
and back.

Printer's hat by Al Koenig and Mike Modrako (USA)

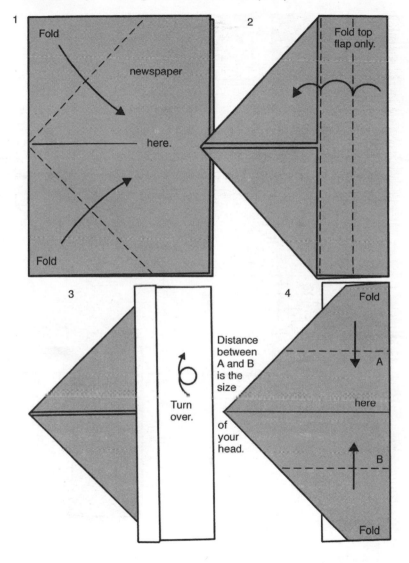

1

Fold

newspaper

here.

Fold

2

Fold top flap only.

3

Turn over.

4

Distance between A and B is the size of your head.

Fold

A

here

B

Fold

Published in the *New Phoenix*, New York.

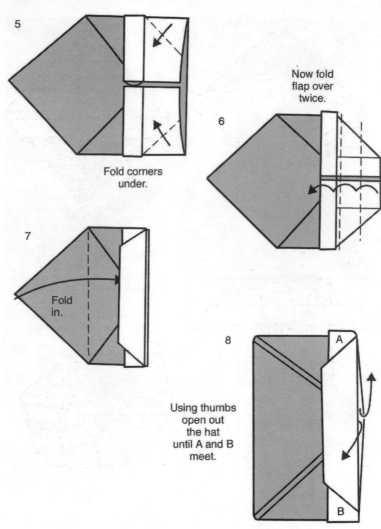

5

Fold corners under.

6

Now fold flap over twice.

7

Fold in.

8

Using thumbs open out the hat until A and B meet.

A

B

By kind permission of the editor, Jay Marshall.

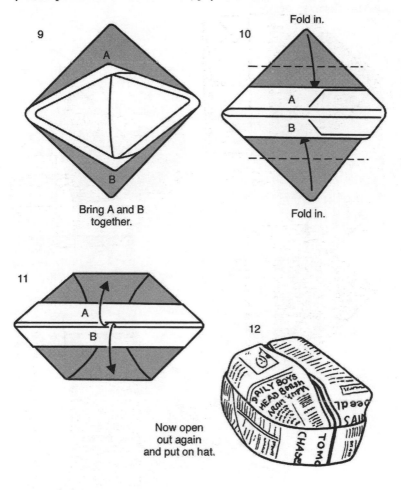

9

A

B

Bring A and B together.

10

Fold in.

A

B

Fold in.

11

A

B

Now open out again and put on hat.

12

Decoration 1 by Robert Harbin (London)
See Multiform to begin.

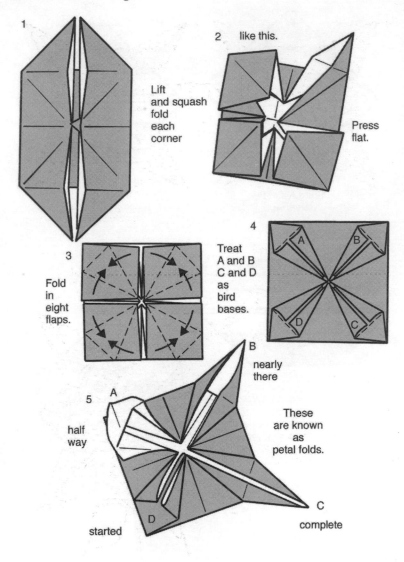

1

Lift
and squash
fold
each
corner

2   like this.

Press
flat.

3

Fold
in
eight
flaps.

4

Treat
A and B
C and D
as
bird
bases.

A   B

D   C

B

nearly
there

5   A

half
way

These
are known
as
petal folds.

C

D

started   complete

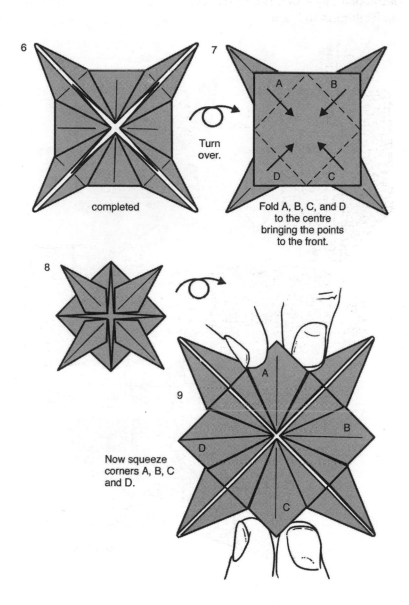

6

Turn over.

completed

7

A   B

D   C

Fold A, B, C, and D
to the centre
bringing the points
to the front.

8

9

A

B

D

C

Now squeeze
corners A, B, C
and D.

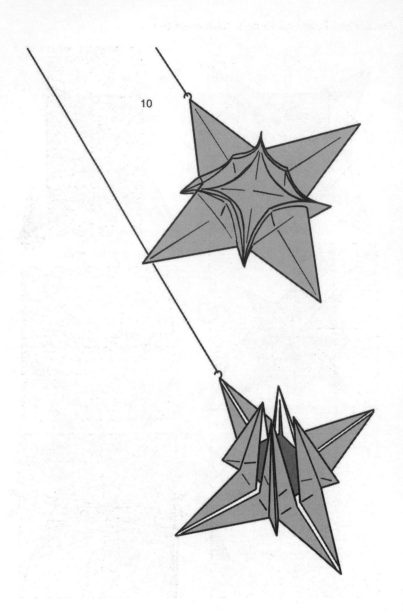

Decoration 2: several folders discovered this

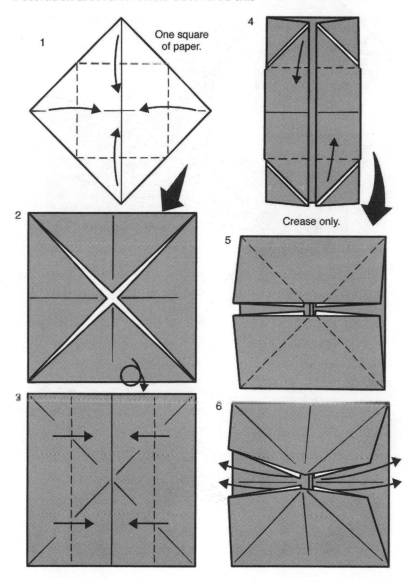

1   One square of paper.

2

3

4

Crease only.

5

6

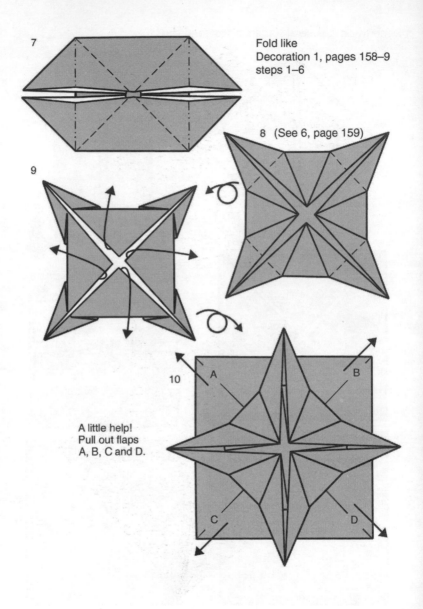

7

Fold like
Decoration 1, pages 158–9
steps 1–6

8 (See 6, page 159)

9

10

A little help!
Pull out flaps
A, B, C and D.

A   B

C   D

162

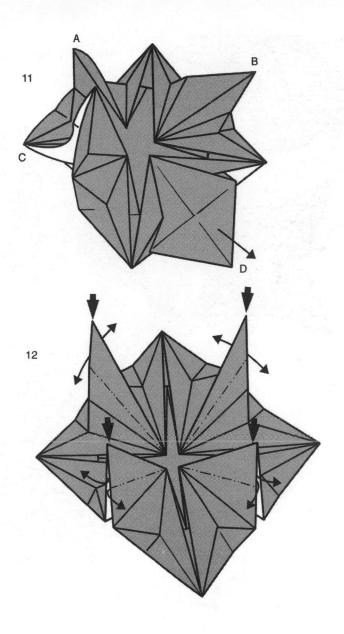

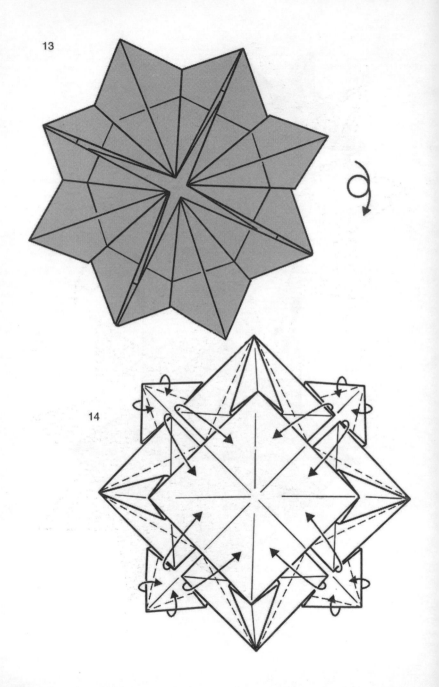

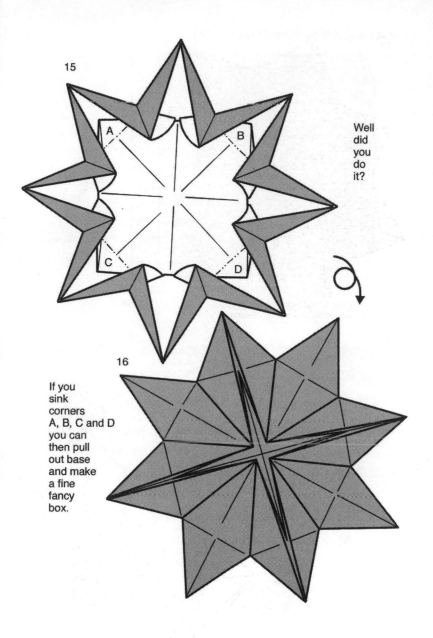

15

A

B

Well
did
you
do
it?

C

D

16

If you
sink
corners
A, B, C and D
you can
then pull
out base
and make
a fine
fancy
box.

Frisbee and star by Robert Neale (USA)

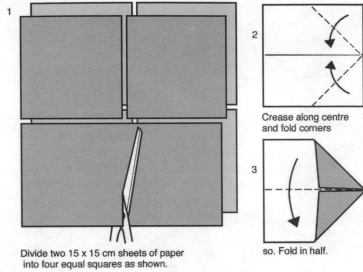

2 Crease along centre and fold corners

3 so. Fold in half.

1 Divide two 15 x 15 cm sheets of paper into four equal squares as shown.

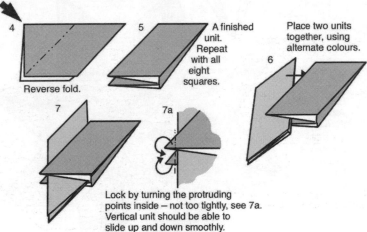

4 Reverse fold.

5 A finished unit. Repeat with all eight squares.

Place two units together, using alternate colours.

6

7

7a Lock by turning the protruding points inside – not too tightly, see 7a. Vertical unit should be able to slide up and down smoothly.

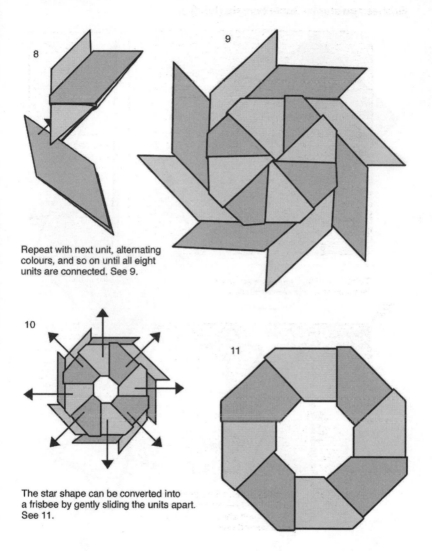

Repeat with next unit, alternating colours, and so on until all eight units are connected. See 9.

The star shape can be converted into a frisbee by gently sliding the units apart. See 11.

Japanese gentleman by Robert Harbin (London)

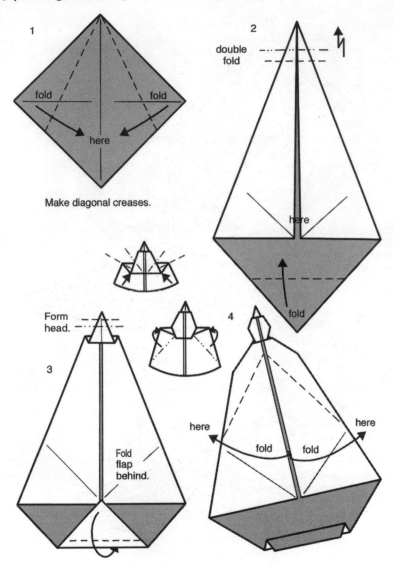

1 fold   fold
here

Make diagonal creases.

2 double
fold

here

fold

3 Form
head.

Fold
flap
behind.

4 here   here

fold   fold

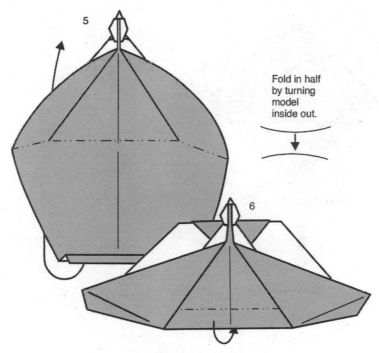

5

Fold in half
by turning
model
inside out.

6

Fold along marked line only.

When you fold flaps
A and B will move upwards.

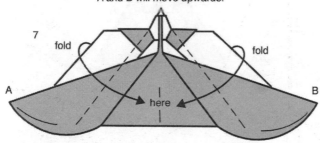

7

fold

fold

A

B

here

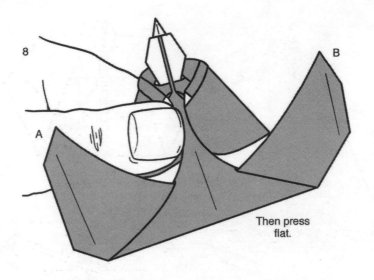

8

A

B

Then press
flat.

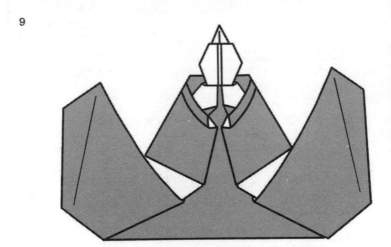

9

Japanese lady

Begin as for the gentleman.

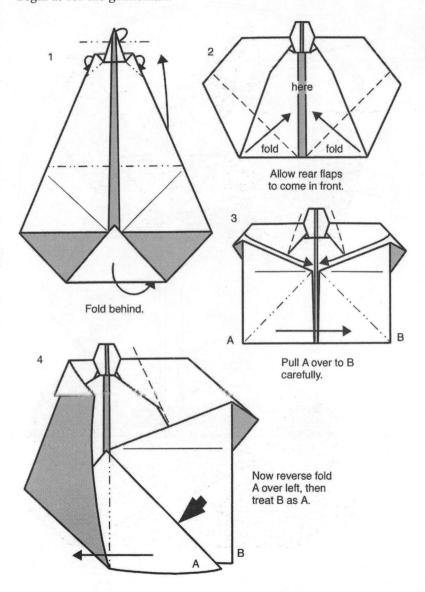

1

Fold behind.

2

here

fold   fold

Allow rear flaps
to come in front.

3

A   B

Pull A over to B
carefully.

4

Now reverse fold
A over left, then
treat B as A.

B

A

5

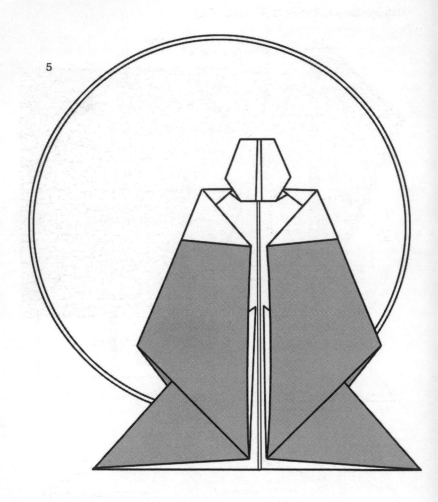

Fish by Samuel Randlett (Illinois, USA)

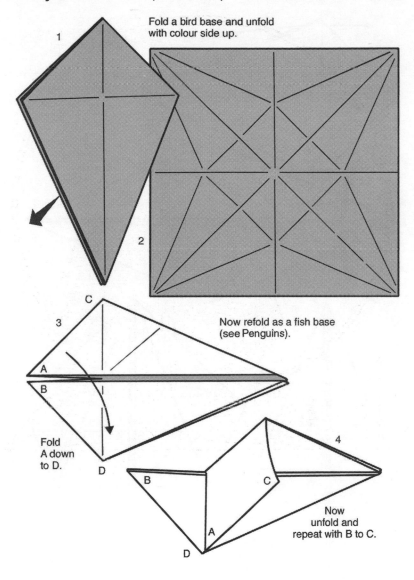

Fold a bird base and unfold with colour side up.

1

2

Now refold as a fish base (see Penguins).

3

C

A

B

Fold A down to D.

D

4

B

C

A

D

Now unfold and repeat with B to C.

Based on the Japanese lady.

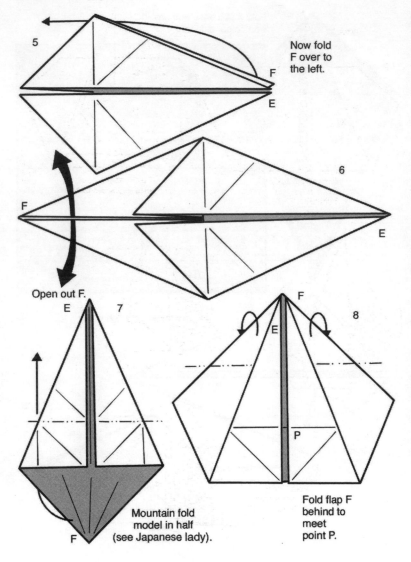

Now fold
F over to
the left.

Open out F.

Mountain fold
model in half
(see Japanese lady).

Fold flap F
behind to
meet
point P.

174

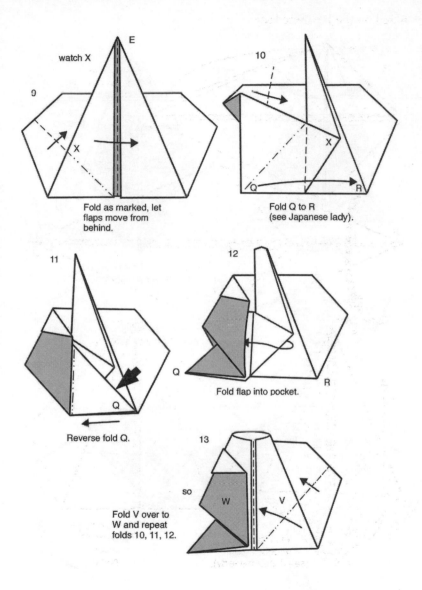

9 watch X

E

X

Fold as marked, let flaps move from behind.

10

X

Q R

Fold Q to R (see Japanese lady).

11

Q

Reverse fold Q.

12

Q R

Fold flap into pocket.

13

so

W V

Fold V over to W and repeat folds 10, 11, 12.

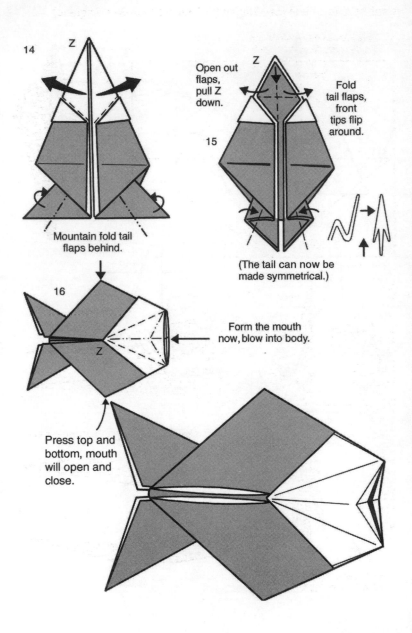

14

Z

Open out
flaps,
pull Z
down.

Z

Fold
tail flaps,
front
tips flip
around.

15

Mountain fold tail
flaps behind.

(The tail can now be
made symmetrical.)

16

Z

Form the mouth
now, blow into body.

Press top and
bottom, mouth
will open and
close.

Ornithonimus by Sidney French (St Leonard's-on-Sea, England)

1 Start from white side of paper.
   Cut diamond from 4 x 3 rectangle.

crease   first

angles   equal

2

Form this shape.

Mountain

3

4

head

fore legs

5

the tail

6

leg   leg

7

Open tail from below to make crimps.

8

tail

Cut both sides
of middle for legs.

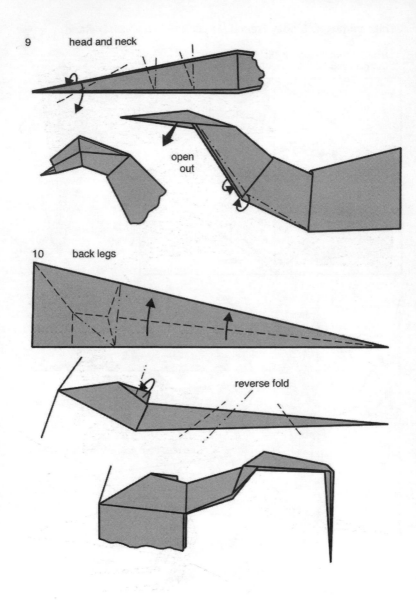

9   head and neck

open
out

10   back legs

reverse fold

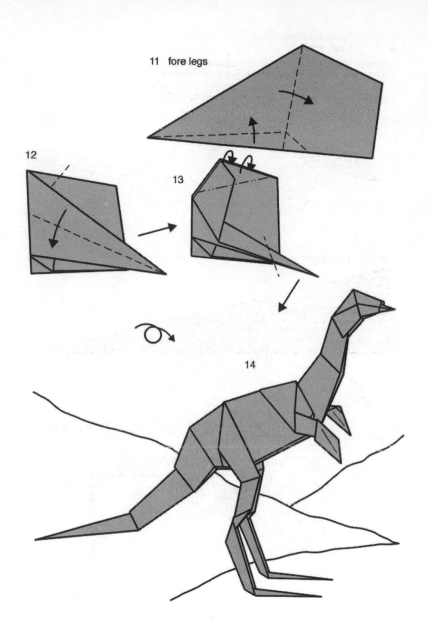

11 fore legs

12

13

14

Aladdin's lamp by Neal Elias (Ohio, USA)

1 A rectangle cut as shown (gold side under).

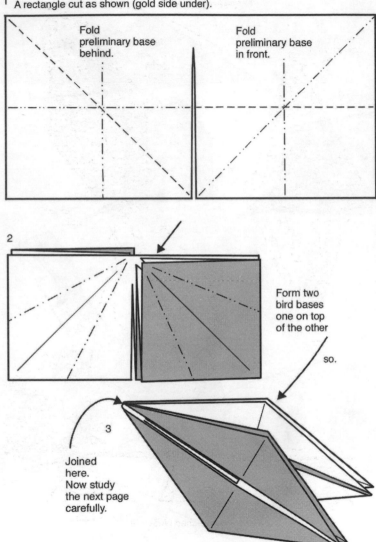

Fold preliminary base behind.

Fold preliminary base in front.

2

Form two bird bases one on top of the other

so.

3

Joined here. Now study the next page carefully.

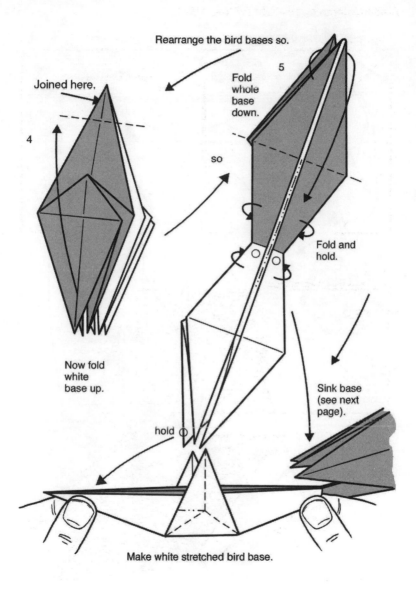

Rearrange the bird bases so.

Joined here.

4

5

Fold whole base down.

so

Fold and hold.

Now fold white base up.

Sink base (see next page).

hold

Make white stretched bird base.

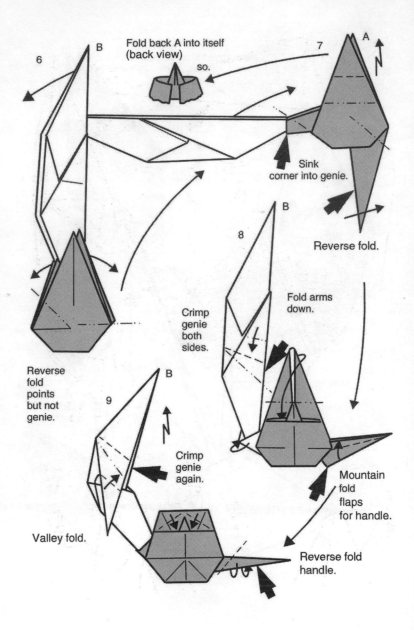

6

B

Fold back A into itself
(back view)

so.

7

A

Sink
corner into genie.

Reverse fold.

Crimp
genie
both
sides.

B

8

Fold arms
down.

Reverse
fold
points
but not
genie.

B

9

Crimp
genie
again.

Mountain
fold
flaps
for handle.

Valley fold.

Reverse fold
handle.

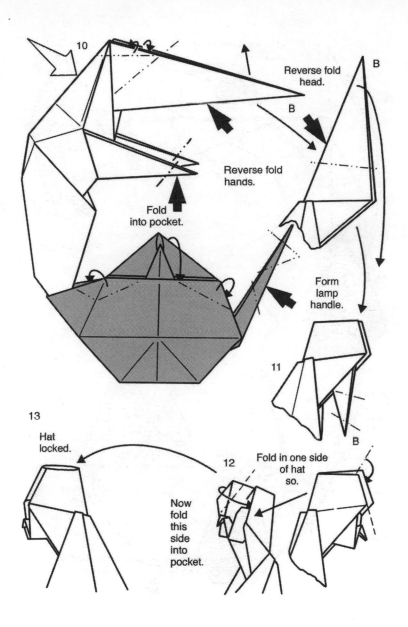

10

Reverse fold
head.

B

B

Reverse fold
hands.

Fold
into pocket.

Form
lamp
handle.

11

13

Hat
locked.

Now
fold
this
side
into
pocket.

12

Fold in one side
of hat
so.

B

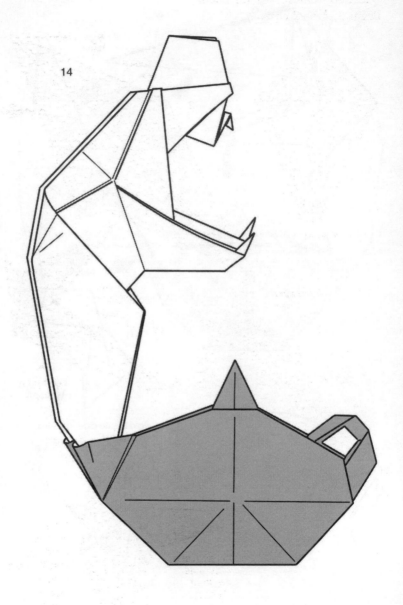

14

Ostrich by Robert Harbin (London)

Begin with bird base.

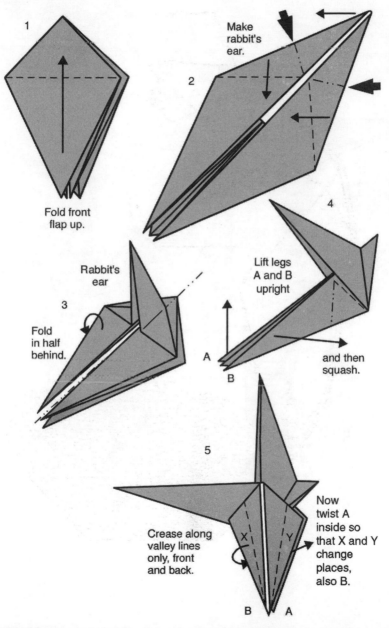

1

Fold front
flap up.

2

Make
rabbit's
ear.

3

Rabbit's
ear

Fold
in half
behind.

4

Lift legs
A and B
upright

A

B

and then
squash.

5

Crease along
valley lines
only, front
and back.

X   Y

Now
twist A
inside so
that X and Y
change
places,
also B.

B   A

Complete with rider.

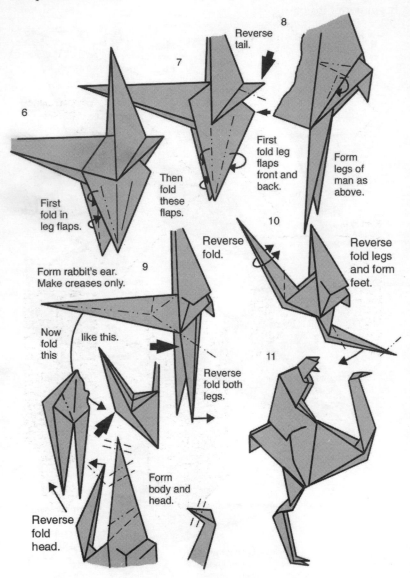

6

First fold in leg flaps.

7

Then fold these flaps.

Reverse tail.

First fold leg flaps front and back.

8

Form legs of man as above.

9

Reverse fold.

Form rabbit's ear. Make creases only.

10

Reverse fold legs and form feet.

Now fold this

like this.

Reverse fold both legs.

11

Reverse fold head.

Form body and head.

Church by Iris Walker (Hull, England)

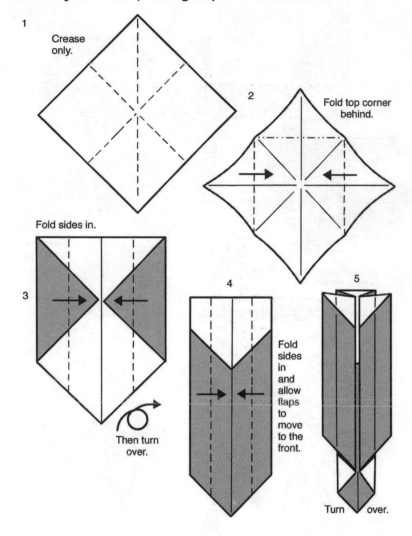

1 Crease only.

2 Fold top corner behind.

3 Fold sides in.

Then turn over.

4 Fold sides in and allow flaps to move to the front.

5 Turn over.

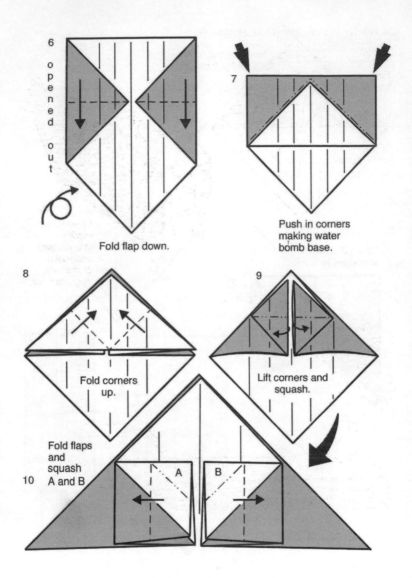

6

opened out

Fold flap down.

7

Push in corners
making water
bomb base.

8

Fold corners
up.

9

Lift corners and
squash.

10 Fold flaps
and
squash
A and B

A

B

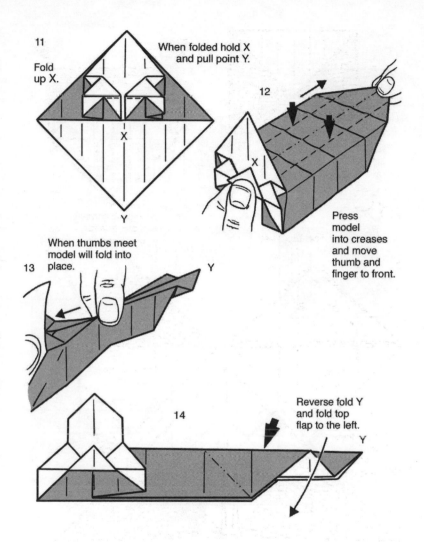

11

Fold up X.

When folded hold X and pull point Y.

X

Y

12

Press model into creases and move thumb and finger to front.

X

13 When thumbs meet model will fold into place.

Y

14

Reverse fold Y and fold top flap to the left.

Y

Y

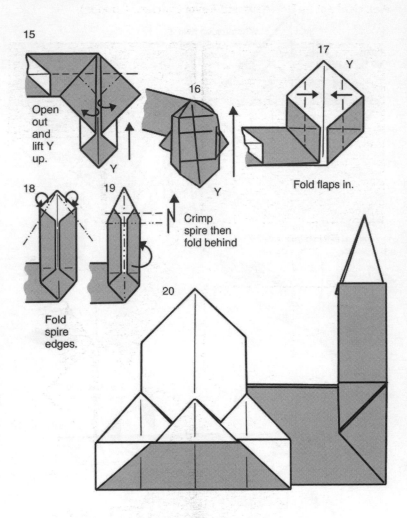

15

Open out and lift Y up.

Y

16

Y

17

Y

Fold flaps in.

18

Fold spire edges.

19

N

Crimp spire then fold behind

20

Pink elephant by Tim Ward and Trevor Hatchett (London)

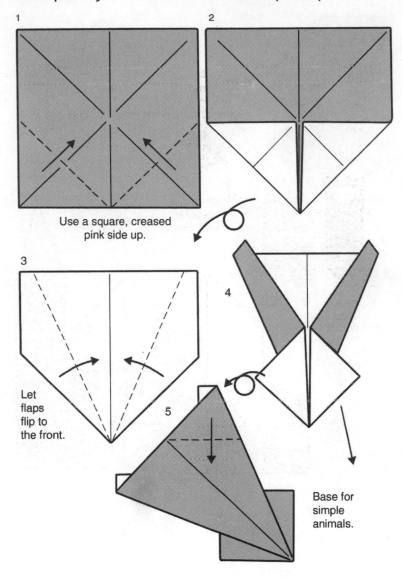

1

Use a square, creased pink side up.

2

3

Let flaps flip to the front.

4

5

Base for simple animals.

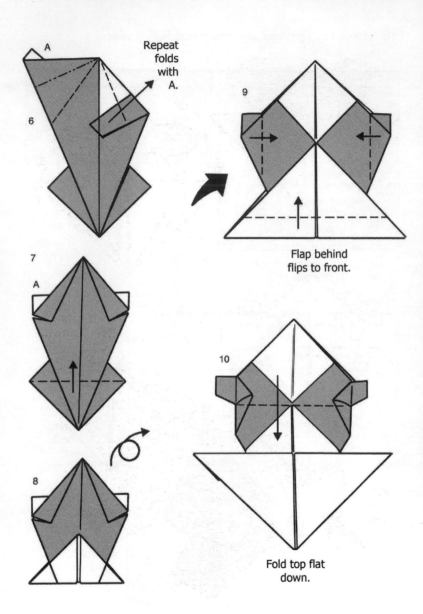

6

A

Repeat folds with A.

9

Flap behind flips to front.

7

A

8

10

Fold top flat down.

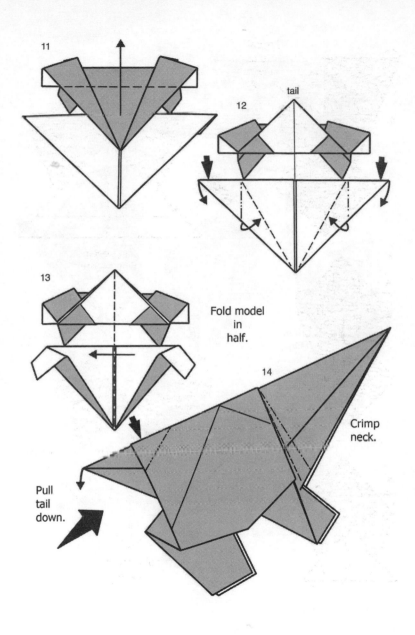

11

12 tail

13

Fold model
in
half.

14

Crimp
neck.

Pull
tail
down.

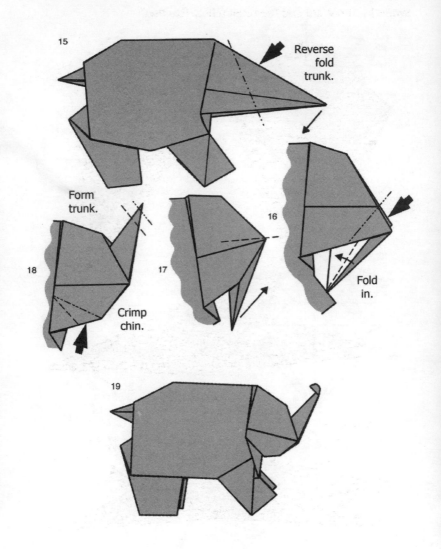

15

Reverse
fold
trunk.

Form
trunk.

16

18

17

Crimp
chin.

Fold
in.

19

Swans by Tim Ward and Trevor Hatchett (London)

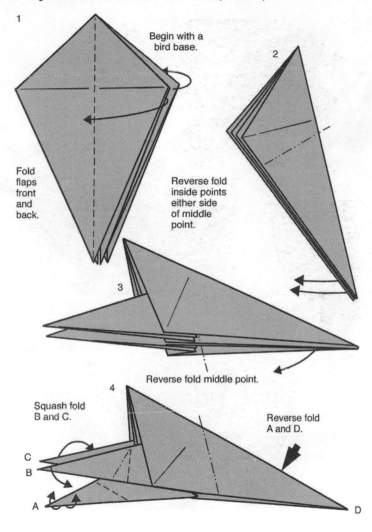

1

Begin with a bird base.

2

Fold flaps front and back.

Reverse fold inside points either side of middle point.

3

Reverse fold middle point.

4

Squash fold B and C.

Reverse fold A and D.

C
B

A

D

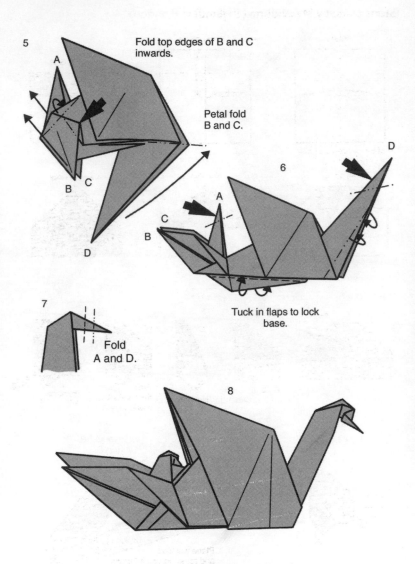

5

A

B C

D

Fold top edges of B and C
inwards.

Petal fold
B and C.

6

C

A

B

D

Tuck in flaps to lock
base.

7

Fold
A and D.

8

Stunt plane by Max Hulme (England)

1 Crease.

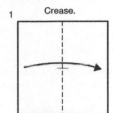

Mark centre point with a small pinch.

2 Fold top down

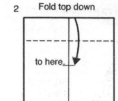

to here.

3 Fold corners in.

4 Fold again

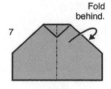

5 like this.

Turn over.

6 Fold down top

to centre point.

7 Fold behind.

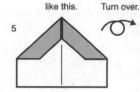

8 Fold down.

Do the same behind

9 like this.

10

Fold then unfold to mark crease.

11

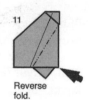

Reverse fold.

12 Curl wing tips.

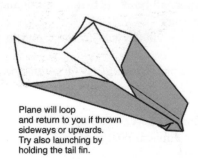

Plane will loop and return to you if thrown sideways or upwards. Try also launching by holding the tail fin.

Taking it further

Bibliography

Here is a list of recommended books for further study. Even if some of these may not be in print, it is worth tracking them down through your local library or second hand bookshop. Any other titles by all of these authors are also strongly recommended. Most of these books are in English. However, do not be put off by an origami book in any other language, as the symbols commonly used are standard, like a kind of Esperanto! You should therefore be able to make the models illustrated if you have understood the symbols within this book.

Biddle, Steve and Megumi *Origami Inspired by Japanese Prints*
British Museum Press, 1998.

Brill, David *Brilliant Origami*
Japan Publications, 1996.

British Origami Society
Many small booklets featuring origami designs, theory, and techniques.
Available via www.britishorigami.org.uk

Fuse, Tomoko *Fabulous Origami Boxes*
Japan Publications, 1998.

Harbin, Robert *Secrets of Origami*
Dover Publications, 1997.

Jackson, Paul *Encyclopaedia of Origami and Papercraft Techniques*
Quarto/Headline Book Publishing, 1991.

Kasahara, Kunihiko *Origami Omnibus*
Japan Publications, 1988.

Kenneway, Eric *Complete Origami*
Ebury Press, 1987.

Lafosse, Michael *Origamido*
Rockport Publishers, 2000.

Lang, Robert *Origami in Action*
St Martin's Press, 1997.

Neale, Robert *Folding Money Fooling*
Kaufman & Co, 1997.

Momotani, Yoshihide and Sumiko *Little Red Riding Hood Origami Picture Book*
Japanese text with some sub-titles.

Montroll, John *North American Animals in Origami*
Dover, 1995.

Shafer, Jeremy *Origami to Astonish and Amuse*
St Martin's Press, 2001.

Takahama, Toshie *Creative Life with Creative Origami*
Mako-Sha. Japanese text with some sub-titles.

Yoshizawa, Akira *Creative Origami*
NHK, 1984. Japanese text.

Origami Internet sites and links

There are a multitude of origami Internet sites, and the following are excellent at showing the vast scope of origami, as well as being good starting points for 'surfing'.

Joseph Wu's Origami page: www.origami.as
Oriland: www.oriland.com
David Mitchell's Origami Heaven: www.mizushobai.freeserve.co.uk
Origami mailing list: origami.kvi.nl

Origami organizations

It is impossible to list all origami organizations, but the following
are strongly recommended: they are well established and efficient.
If you join, you will certainly increase your knowledge and skills
in origami. All of these societies produce quality magazines
with diagrams for new origami designs. As with origami books
in other languages (even Japanese!), the accepted usage of the
standard symbols by these international origami societies means
that you should successfully be able to fold the models which are
diagrammed in their publications. Use the addresses or websites
detailed below to find out how you can join, and to obtain more
general information.

These organizations organize, at least once a year, a residential
convention for origami enthusiasts – well worth attending if you
can. There is no doubt that the best way to learn about origami is
to meet and communicate with others who share your interest.

British Origami Society
2a The Chestnuts
Countesthorpe
Leicester
LE85TL
UK
www.britishorigami.info

Nippon Origami Association
2-064 Domir Gobancho
12 Gobancho, Chiyoda-ku
Tokyo 102-0076
JAPAN
member.nifty.ne.jp/noanet/
english/english.htm

**Asociación Española de
Papiroflexia**
13156 - 28080 Madrid
SPAIN
www.pajarita.org

Origami USA
15 West 77 Street, New York
NY10024-5192
USA
www.origami-usa.org

Centro Diffusione Origami
Casella postale 42
21040 Caronno Varesino
 (VA)
ITALY
www.origami-cdo.it

Japan Origami Academic Society
c/o Gallery Origami House
1-33-8-216, Hakusan
Bunkyo-ku, Tokyo
113-0001, JAPAN
www.origami.gr.jp

Stockists of origami books and paper

In addition to the origami societies detailed above, the following
supply good selections of origami books and paper. These are
available by mail order, or via the Internet.

Book Ends
25–8 Thurloe Place, South Kensington, London SW7 2HQ
www.worthhall.demon.co.uk/supplies/bookends

Sasuga Japanese Bookstore
7 Upland Road, Cambridge, MA 02140 USA
www.sasugabooks.com

Kim's Crane Origami Supplies
P.O. Box 222971, Chantilly, VA 20153-2971 USA
www.kimscrane.com

Viereck-Verlag
Postfach 1922, Freising, Germany
www.viereck-verlag.de

Credits